D1200149

# Berlin 1945

The collapse of the 'Thousand-Year' Reich

# Berlin 1945

## The collapse of the 'Thousand-Year' Reich

D. STAVROPOULOS - S. VOURLIOTIS - J. TERNIOTIS
I. KOTOULAS - S. VALMAS - G. ZOURIDIS

*'A Hopeless Defense, Berlin, April 1945' by Johnny Shumate.*

**AUTHORS**
D. Stavropoulos - S. Vourliotis - J. Terniotis
I. Kotoulas - S. Valmas - G. Zouridis

**EDITORS** (ENGLISH EDITION)
Ioannis Theodoratos
Stelios Demiras

**TRANSLATOR**
Alexis Mehtidis

**PROOF EDITOR**
Soultana Kalligas

**COVER ART AND UNIFORM RESEARCH-ILLUSTRATIONS**
Johnny Shumate

**AIRCRAFT PROFILES**
Vincenzo Auletta

**AFV PROFILES**
Dimitris Hadoulas

**ART DIRECTOR AND COVER DESIGN**
Dimitra Mitsou

**MAPS**
Dimitra Mitsou

**PICTURE CREDITS**
Bunderarchiv, US Archives, Authors' Archives,
Periscopio Publications' Collection

First published in Greece in 2009
by Periscopio Publications
in cooperation with Squadron/Signal Publications

Distributed worldwide exclusively
by Squadron/Signal Publications
1115 Crowley Drive
Carrollton, TX 75006-1312 U.S.A.
www.SquadronSignalPublications.com

© 2009 Periscopio Publications

*All rights reserved. Reproduction in part or in whole
is forbidden without prior written permission from the publisher,
except in case of brief quotations used in reviews.*

**ISBN:** 978-0-89747-568-6

---

**DIMITRIOS STAVROPOULOS**
Dimitrios Stavropoulos is a graduate
mechanical engineer and works in the
Greek defense industry. He has published
a series of articles on military history since
1996 and has edited 20 books in the Greek
language.

**SOTIRIS VOURLIOTIS**
Sotiris Vourliotis was born in Athens in
1968. He studied in the Department of
Mechanical Engineering of the Chalkis
Technological Educational Institution and
then in the School of Mechanical
Engineering of the National Technical
University of Athens.
He works as a public works designer.
He has written articles for the Periscopio
Publications' military history and defence
magazines since 2000 and has dealt with
various subjects, mostly of the World War
II period for which he has been interested
since his school years.

**JOHN TERNIOTIS**
John Terniotis was born in Athens on
September 1952 and studied Aircraft
Engineering. After some years of military
service with the Hellenic Army Armoured
Corps, he joined Civil Aviation and still
works as Maintenance Operations Chief
Inspector. He has written several articles
on Military History issues, and performed
photographic research in WWII
battlefields, airfields and other sites in

Greece. His hobby is Aviation Archaeology.
He owns a collection of several relics of
Luftwaffe and Regia Aeronautica aircraft
and items found in areas used by the Axis
forces during WWII.

**IOANNIS KOTOULAS**
Ioannis Kotoulas is a historian and was
born in Sydney, Australia, in 1976. He
studied history and archaeology at the
National University of Athens and has an
M.A. in the History of Art. He is currently
writing his dissertation on *Neogothic
Tradition in European Architecture and in
Greece* at the same university. He is the
scientific editor and translator of the series
*Historical Archives of World War II* (Athens,
Periplous Publications, 2007). Six of his
monographs, titled *Vikings*, *The
Peloponnesian War*, *The Army of Alexander the
Great*, *Josef Stalin*, *The Rise of the Third Reich*,
and *Axis War Crimes*, have been published
by Periscopio Publications, and *Intellectuals
and Power*, was published by Periplous
Publications. Many of his articles have been
published in various historical magazines
by Periscopio Publications and in the
Sunday editions of the newspaper Vima.

**STAVROS VALMAS**
Stavros Valmas was born in Athens, Greece in
1964. Educated in the US (Arizona State
University), he has a B.Sc. in Industrial
Engineering and one in Business
Administration. He is Logistics Manager for a

major metals manufacturer in Greece and has
traveled extensively around Europe to visit
military museums. These visits have afforded
him a large picture collection. His main area
of interest is World War II German and
Soviet land and air equipment. Currently,
he is building up his Desert Storm photo
collection.

**GEORGE ZOURIDIS**
George Zouridis was born in Athens, Greece
in 1955. He studied at the Athens University
of Economics and Business, graduating in
1978. Graduate studies followed in Boston,
USA, from where he acquired a Master in
Economics. Zouridis has been dealing with
the study of modern and contemporary
history for more than 20 years and has been
contributing to Periscopio Publications since
1998. He has written several articles as well as
alternative history scenarios about World
War II. He has also written *The October
Revolution 1917* for Periscopio Publications.

# Contents

**8**   The opposing forces in the last Battle
*by G. Zouridis*

**22**   The Battle of Berlin
The collapse of the 'Thousand-Year' Reich (1945)
*by D. Stavropoulos*

**70**   Hanna Reitsch
The last flight to besieged Berlin
*by J. Terniotis*

**80**   The last days of the war in the *Führerbunker*
*by S. Vourliotis*

**96**   Death and ideology in Berlin 1945
*by I. Kotoulas*

**108**   The ideological weapons of the Red Army
Soviet propaganda in the Battle of Berlin
*by I. Kotoulas*

**114**   Soviet and German Order of Battle
*by Tony Le Tissier*

**118**   The opposing commanders
*by D. Stavropoulos*

**121**   Lesser-known details
*by D. Stavropoulos*

**124**   Photofile of the Battle of Berlin
*by S. Valmas*

**128**   Bibliography

*20 April 1945. Hitler awards the Iron Cross to Hitler Youth outside his bunker.*

# Preface

The Western Allies had driven back Hitler's last, desperate effort in the Ardennes by the dawn of 1945. If there were any reason in war, this German defeat should have marked the end of hostilities, but the Allies' insistence on Germany's unconditional surrender deterred the Germans from making even the smallest concession to end the war. British military historian and strategist J. F. C. Fuller opposed the concept of unconditional surrender, saying said that Hitler, like Samson, only had the option of "dying with the barbarians," letting Germany's ruins fall upon them, upon himself, and upon the German people. The fanatical Nazis were the only ones who did not want to understand that the war had been lost for Germany. But it had become clear that another kind of war was right around the corner: the war between the Americans, British, and Soviets for Europe's domination after Germany's defeat. With the Soviets having reached Budapest and the Oder River, it was clear who would dominate Eastern Europe. The only hope for the Americans and the British to retain what they could from central Europe was to take Berlin. But the 'Russian steamroller' forestalled them. Colossal Soviet forces attacked the capital of the 'Thousand-Year' Reich in April 1945. The last act of the confrontation between the Communists and the National Socialists and the first act of the Cold War would take place there, amidst the rubble of the destroyed city.

**Nikos Giannopoulos**
*Historian*

# The opposing forces in the last Battle

*'A Hopeless Defense, Berlin, April 1945.'* In the last days of Battle of Berlin remnants of various units tried to stop the Russian offensive to the center of the capital of Germany. A panzer officer (Scharführer) armed with an MP40 submachine gun along with two soldiers of the Waffen-SS, armed with Gewehr 43 and MG 42, are trying to stop the Russian advance into the heart of the city of Berlin. (Painting by Johnny Shumate)

On 16 April 1945, 22,000 Soviet guns opened fire against German positions in the outskirts of Berlin. The last great battle that would judge Third Reich's destiny had just begun. The Soviets took part in this confrontation with 2,500,000 troops, supported by 6,300 armored vehicles and 8,400 aircraft. Opposite them were 500,000 German troops, 75,000 Hitler Youth (*Hitler-Jugend*) troops and Peoples' Militia (*Volkssturm*) forces. The Germans fought in a superhuman way, driven by the power of despair, although the fight was more than uneven. On 4 May the Battle of Berlin was over with the city's capture by the Soviets.

## The Soviet Army

Three men planned the final arrangements for the Battle of Berlin on 3 April 1945 in the large conference hall of the Kremlin. Josef Stalin listened carefully to Field Marshal Georgy Konstantinovich Zhukov, a short, sturdy 49-year-old man, the victor of the Battle of Moscow and the main actor in the victory in Kursk, and Field Marshal Ivan Stepanovich Konev, a tall 48-year-old man, who had distinguished himself in the Battle of Kursk and in Operation 'Bagration' in 1944 that broke up the German Army Group

Center and drove the Red Army to Berlin's outskirts. At the end of the meeting, Stalin set the date for the Battle of Berlin for 16 April 1945. This date was top-secret information and was given to the field marshals orally.

The two field marshals rushed to their fronts' headquarters. They had to reorganize and strengthen the Soviet forces, though not much time was left for the beginning of the battle. It is characteristic that many of Field Marshal Zhukov's rifle divisions numbered only 3,200 men, while their strength, according to the table of organization, was for 12,000 men.

*ISU-152 self-propelled gun armed with a 152 mm. Assigned to Field Marshal Konev's forces operating in Berlin in April 1945. The ISU-152 and the ISU-122, were organized into independent, heavy, self-propelled gun regiments that attacked fortified positions, tanks, and vehicles and supported the infantry. Finished in Russian Green. (Illustration by Dimitris Hadoulas / Historical Notes by Stelios Demiras)*

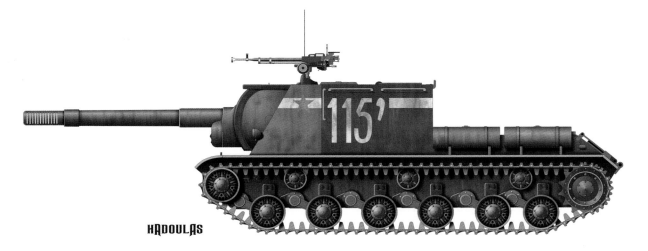

*Katyusha **rocket** launchers bombarding Berlin.*

Finally, 140 Soviet divisions (assigned to 29 armies), numbering 2,500,000 men, 6,300 armored vehicles and 41,600 guns of various calibers were arrayed on the banks of the Oder River, the last natural barrier before Berlin. Three Soviet fronts were to attack Berlin: the 1st Belorussian Front (Field Marshal Zhukov), 1st Ukrainian (Field Marshal Ivan Konev) and 2nd Belorussian (Field Marshal Konstantin Konstantinovich Rokossovsky).

# 1st Belorussian Front

This front was under the command of Field Marshal Georgy Zhukov and had nine armies and two tank armies. Its total strength was 768,100 men, supported by 11,000 guns and 5,000 mortars. In addition, 400 rocket launchers, the renowned *Katyusha* as the Soviets called them, would support it. The Germans called them *Stalin Orgel* (Stalin Organ), alluding to the sound of the weapon's rockets. There

were 3,500 tanks available in the 1st Belorussian Front, including self-propelled guns and tank destroyers.

Zhukov's forces, constituting the main axis of advance of the Soviet attack against Berlin, were to cross the Oder River and capture the Seelow Heights. The Germans had taken care to fortify and place a large number of 88 mm anti-tank guns on the heights. Zhukov asked for 143 powerful anti-aircraft searchlights from Moscow. When the attack would start they would operate to blind the German defenders of the Seelow Heights

In the 3 April meeting, and with Stalin's approval, Zhukov asked Georgy Malenkov, Minister of Supply and a member of the Soviet Union Defense Council, for the number of guns in his front area to increase to 295 per kilometer (one tube per 3 meters!). From 25 April onwards the 1st Belorussian Front was strengthened with 11,000 guns and so Field Marshal Zhukov finally had 22,000 guns at his disposal.

The 1st Belorussian Front was composed of the following formations:
● The 8th Guards Army, an elite formation of the Red Army, under the command of 45-year old Colonel General Vasily Ivanovich Chuikov. He had distinguished himself as a Red Army colonel during the Russian Civil War in the Siberian front. He had been commander of the Soviet forces in the Battle of Stalingrad in 1942 and had been infected with a skin disease in the neck and the hands, due to a heavy psychological burden. This had not been fully cured by April 1945 and general Chuikov was wearing black gloves during the Battle of Berlin.
● The 1st Guards Tank Army (Colonel General Mikhail Yefimovich Katukov, a veteran of Operation 'Bagration' in

*Soviet troops preparing for the assault on the Chancellery.*

1944) was positioned on the 8th Army's eastern end. The 65th Tank Brigade was the army's vanguard and it would try to capture the Seelow Heights.

● The 3rd Shock Army (Colonel General Vasily Ivanovich Kuznetsov, a veteran of the Battle of Kursk) was in the center. It has to be noted that units from this army (the 171st, 150th, and 207th Rifle Divisions of the 79th Rifle Corps) took part in the final assault for the Reich Chancellery on 2 May 1945.

● The 5th Shock Army (Colonel General Nikolai Erastovich Berzarin) was arrayed to the left of the 3rd Army. Lieutenant General Berzarin was posted as Commandant of Berlin on 26 April.

● The 47th Army (Lieutenant General F. Perkhorovich) was to the north of the 3rd Shock Army.

● The 3rd Army (Colonel General A. Gorbatov).

● The 33rd Army (Colonel General V. D. Tsvetaev).

● The 69th Army (Colonel General V. Kolpakchi).

● The 1st Polish Army (Lieutenant General S. Poplawski).

● The 61st Army (Lieutenant General P. Belov).

● Finally, the 2nd Guards Tank Army (Colonel General S. Bogdanov) was placed in the northern end of Field Marshal Zhukov's forces.

The casualties of Zhukov's forces were at least 100,000 men.

## 1st Ukrainian Front

This front finally fielded seven rifle armies, two tank armies and units of other formations with a total strength of 511,700 men. Its commander was Field Marshal Ivan Konev, a commissar in the Red Army during the Civil War. Konev had become a member of the regular army in 1926 as a colonel. His past in the Communist Party made professional soldiers, like Zhukov, dislike him.

The Ukrainian Front's mission was to support Zhukov's forces in their attacking operation. If the Belorussian Front would meet obstacles, Konev had Stalin's permission to capture Berlin first, something the capable and ambitious field marshal yearned for.

Field Marshal Konev asked for reinforcements for the 1st Ukrainian Front in the 3 April meeting. Josef Stalin promised the 28th and the 31st Armies a strength of 300,000 men, who were sent on 27 April during the last stages of the Battle of Berlin. He had 11,000 guns and 5,000 mortars, but asked for another 11,000 guns as his artillery strength was inferior to Zhukov's. He received the artillery reinforcements on 22 April.

The 1st Ukrainian Front's order of battle was the following:
● 13th Army (Colonel General N. Pukhov).
● 3rd Guards Army (Colonel General V. Gordov).
● 5th Guards Army (Colonel General A. Zhadov).
● 52nd Army (Colonel General K. Koroteyev).
● 2nd Polish Army (Lieutenant General K. Swierczewski).
● 3rd Guards Tank Army (Colonel General P. Rybalko, a veteran of the Battle of Kursk)

● 28th Army (Lieutenant General A. Luchinsky).
● 4th Guards Tank Army (Colonel General D. Lelyushenko).
● 31st Army (Lieutenant General V. Baranov).

Konev's men were ready on 2 May 1945 for the final attack to capture the Chancellery. An urgent order by Stalin called this attack off and allowed the forces of his rival, Field Marshal Zhukov, to win the laurels of the final victory. Field Marshal Konev felt deeply bitter and disappointed. One of Konev's objectives, though, was to meet the American forces in the area of Torgau, on the banks of river Elbe, and he accomplished that on 25 April 1945.

Field Marshal Konev admitted in an interview given in Moscow in 1963 to British journalist Cornelius Ryan that his forces had 150,000 casualties (dead and seriously wounded).

## 2nd Belorussian Front

This front was under Field Marshal Konstantin Rokossovsky with a strength of 314,000 men and it played a secondary role in the Battle of Berlin. It kept the German forces of the 3rd Panzer Army (*Panzer-Armee*), under General Hasso von Manteuffel, occupied, not letting them strengthen Berlin's defenses.

*Soviet Joseph Stalin 2 (JS-2) heavy tank, 11th Tank Corps, Red Army. Used during the final attack in Berlin in April 1945, as well as during its occupation. Allied air superiority meant that ground forces had to carry air recognition signs. In this case it consists of a white cross on the turret and dotted white bands around the turret. The powerful 122 mm gun distinguished the JS-2 as the indisputable winner of tank battles since the beginning of 1945, when it first appeared on the battlefield, to the end of the war. Finished in Russian Green. (Illustration by Dimitris Hadoulas / Historical Notes by Stelios Demiras)*

HADOULAS

The 2st Belorussian Front's order of battle was the following:
- 2nd Shock Army (Colonel General I. Fedyurinsky).
- 65th Army (Colonel General P. Batov).
- 70th Army (Colonel General V. Popov).
- 49th Army (Colonel General I. Grishin).
- 19th Army
- and 5th Guards Tank Army.

## The Soviet rifle division

The Red Army, following Czarist tradition, named its infantry divisions as rifle (*streltsy*) divisions, believing that it gave them a sense of importance compared to the term infantry (*piekhoty*) division. Each rifle division was composed of three regiments, each of three battalions. Each rifle battalion had three companies.

Each rifle division had a theoretical strength, in December 1944, of 11,706 men, 1,200 draught horses and 342 vehicles. Its firepower was 6,330 rifles, 3,594 submachine guns, 166 heavy machine guns and 127 infantry mortars. Heavy support weapons were fifty-four 45 mm anti-tank guns, twelve 37mm anti-aircraft guns, forty-four 76 mm field guns and twenty 122 mm howitzers. The superiority of the Soviet rifle division

in firepower is clear compared to a German, British or American infantry division.

The need to support the Soviet tank corps led to the creation of mechanized rifle divisions. Their table of organization was similar to the typical rifle divisions, but they were equipped with more DP light machine guns. These formations were not equipped with any armored personnel carriers, though, as were the similar German, American or British divisions. Their riflemen rode on tanks, exposed to enemy fire and sustained heavy casualties as a consequence.

The company of a typical rifle division had three rifle platoons and one machine gun platoon. The rifle company had a total of three water-cooled Maxim machine guns, nine DP light machine guns, 85 rifles,

*Soviet riflemen advancing towards the Chancellery.*

*Soviet SU-100 Model 1945 self-propelled gun, 383rd Self-propelled Artillery Regiment, 9th Corps, 3rd Guards Tank Army, 1st Ukrainian Front, Berlin, April 1945. It was one of the most successful self-propelled guns produced by the Soviet Union and was armed with a 100 mm gun on the T-34 hull. Its production began in September 1944 at Uralmashzavod and it soon proved to be a reliable weapon that could face the German Tiger and Panther on equal terms. Finished in Russian Green. (Illustration by Dimitris Hadoulas / Historical Notes by Stelios Demiras)*

*The Reichstag building after the end of the Battle of Berlin. On the foreground, a destroyed German 88 mm gun is visible.*

12 sub-machine guns (usually of the PPSh type) and eight Tokarev pistols. A mechanized rifle company had nine DP light machine guns, 27 rifles, 57 PPSh sub-machine guns and five Tokarev pistols.

The rifle and mechanized rifle divisions that distinguished themselves in the battlefield were renamed as Guards divisions, reviving thus the old Czarist custom. These divisions were better fed, dressed, armed, and paid compared to the rest of the Soviet divisions.

## The Soviet armored formations

The existing Soviet tank divisions were abolished during the winter of 1942 and tank brigades took their place, each of which had a mechanized rifle company, as well. These brigades were like a British or an American armored battalion in size. In the summer of 1942, the Soviets formed tank corps, equivalent to a British or an American armored division. The experience gained by the Soviets during the great battles of

the summer of 1942 made them exercise command of these formations efficiently.

A Soviet tank battalion fielded a KV heavy tank company, a T-34 medium tank company and a T-60 light tank company in the beginning of 1942. In the end of 1944 the Soviet tank battalion had one IS-2 and two T-34/85 tank companies. Some units kept their KV-1 tanks due to a lack of IS-2s. Most of the KV tanks were assigned to independent heavy tank battalions, which were placed under rifle divisions in an infantry support mission. It has to be noted that KV tanks were used in the Battle of Berlin.

Soviet historians diligently do not mention that many of the Soviet tank battalions were equipped with the American-built M4A2 Sherman tank, which was armed with a 76 mm gun. These tanks, as well as thousands of GMC trucks and Jeeps were given by the American government under the Lend-Lease Act, contributing heavily to the Soviet victory.

The Soviet tank crews' training had been inferior compared to the

*German rubble-clearing units during a Soviet bombardment of the city.*

Germans. In addition, the Soviets did not pay any attention to the use of the ground features in deploying their tanks during their crews' training. But the German panzer crews were not being trained so well in 1944 and the Soviets had improved their training by then.

Finally, the Soviet IS-2 tanks, weighing at 46 tons, were equal to the German Panthers and Tigers. Their SU-100, SU-122, ISU-122 and ISU-152 tank destroyers / self-propelled guns were assigned to battalions for use as tank destroyers or as self-propelled artillery to support the taking of the enemy's fortified positions by mechanized rifle units.

## Soviet artillery

Josef Stalin used to call the artillery "queen of the guns" and, indeed, the Soviet Army took great care in its development, when, in the middle of the war, the huge gun losses sustained led to its reorganization. Each rifle division fielded a 76 mm gun regiment and a 122 mm howitzer regiment. The higher caliber guns, organized in artillery divisions, were *Stavka* (under the general command) Reserves, and they were assigned to various armies and fronts, depending on their needs. *Stavka* directly controlled 35 per cent of the Red Army guns in the beginning of 1945.

Thirty artillery divisions and seven Guards mortar divisions had been formed by the end of 1944. These seven divisions were under direct *Stavka* command and were equipped with rocket launchers. They were the preferred support weapons of the Soviet army commanders because their saturated fire could be launched against a specific area in a very short time.

The German military were in awe of the Soviet artillery firepower but they noted that it lacked flexibility in its use. Soviet artillery fire was usually planned for certain hours of the day and for specific front sectors, usually of the frontline, while rear areas were ignored. The German infantry units, on the other hand, having to suffer the Soviet artillery's terrible blows, did not share their staff officers' view.

The Red Army also formed self-propelled artillery units equipped with the ISU-122 and ISU-152 guns, which were assigned to the tank corps. The SU-76 assault guns, on the other hand, were organic to artillery units and were assigned to rifle divisions in order to support their infantry.

## Supply and engineer units

Soviet Army supply units carried out the titanic work of supplying 2,500,000 men with food, fuel, ammunition and equipment. At the same time, on the eve of the Soviet attack in Berlin, they arranged for ammunition reserves to be organized, mostly in artillery shells and tank gun rounds.

Soviet engineers were among the unsung heroes of the Battle of Berlin. Bridging the Oder River with the help of pontoon bridges was accomplished in two hours; it took six hours to build bridges for the Soviet guns and the T-34 tanks to cross the river, and bridges capable of withstanding the weight of the IS-2 tank took 12 hours to build. Soviet engineer troops were fired at fiercely by the German artillery many times, while working on the bridges. Their contribution in the Battle of Berlin was decisive, although underrated.

## The Soviet soldier: Training-Morale

The Soviet soldier was tough, sturdy for the campaign privations and obedient to his superiors' orders. In 1941, the level of training was lower than that of most European armies, though. One of the major disadvantages of the Red Army during 1941-43 was the lack of initiative shown by its non-commissioned officers. There was a qualitative

*German* Jagdpanzer *38(t) Hetzer (Panzerjäger 38(t) mit 7,5 cm Pak 39) tank destroyer. It took part in the operations conducted around the Chancellery in April 1945, along with the 11th SS Volunteer Panzer Grenadier Division 'Nordland' remnants. Its superstructure was built on the successful hull of the Czech PzKpfw 38(t) and was armed with a Pak 39/48 75 mm gun and one MG 34 or MG 42 7.92 mm machine gun. Finished in a three-color scheme with Sand Yellow as the base paint and irregular stripes of Dark Green and Red Brown overpainted. (Illustration by Dimitris Hadoulas / Historical Notes by Stelios Demiras)*

improvement in the army's training from 1944, and efforts were made for the company and platoon commanders to show a spirit of initiative.

Some Soviet poets, such as Ilya Ehrenburg, and other intellectuals implored the Soviet troops not to spare the Germans' lives, and women and babies fell victim to Russian troops seeking to avenge the suffering their country had faced under the German occupation. Even Field Marshal Georgy Zhukov who was usually sparing in his words, urged his soldiers to show no mercy to the inhabitants of the German towns they would capture. So, many Soviet troops were imbued with the feeling of revenge.

The Slavic-descent Soviet soldiers from European Russia were the ones who took on the burden of fighting the war during 1941-44, and who liberated their motherland with their blood. Their morale was high during the Battle of Berlin, but their bravery and enthusiasm gradually gave way to prudence. Capturing Berlin was but a symbolic act, without any strategic significance. No Soviet soldier wished to be the last victim in the last battle of World War II in Europe. Stalin replaced most Soviet Army units' casualties with Kalmuchs, Tatars, Kirghisians, Armenians, Chechenians and Azerbaijanis. These men formed the first assault units and had most of the casualties sustained. The biggest share of the murders, rapes and violence in Berlin against the non-combatant population during and after the battle is attributed to them.

Contrary to what is believed, the Soviet officers that had graduated military schools were highly educated and most of the higher and highest officers spoke German, because they had been taught this language in

military schools. These officers did not commit violence; on the contrary, they stopped the Asiatic-descent Soviet troops under their command from committing further atrocities.

Finally, it is worth mentioning that Field Marshal Konev was an avid bookworm and often surprised his staff officers by reciting excerpts from the works of poets Turgenev and Pushkin.

# The German forces

The Soviets had completed the liberation of Poland by the beginning of December 1944 and had invaded

*Volkssturm **troops and Hitler Youth members armed with the panzerfaust, waiting in their trenches for the Soviet tanks.***

*Sergeant Pyotr Shcherbina (right), one of the first to plant the Soviet flag on the Reichstag building.*

East Prussia. The Germans fielded 99 combat-ready divisions to face them and another 38, under General Otto Wöhler, were in the outskirts of Budapest, Hungary, which was threatened by the Soviets. The Waffen SS elite formations (1st 'Leibstandarte Adolf Hitler', 2nd 'Das Reich' and 3rd 'Totenkopf', all Panzer Grenadier Divisions) were fighting at the side of their reluctant and distrustful Hungarian allies, instead of defending their motherland. Despite General Heinz Guderian's advice to send more divisions to the Eastern Front, Hitler decided to withdraw 62 divisions, which were used in the Battle of the Bulge, and only 37 low strength divisions remained.

In the beginning of 1945 a German infantry division numbered 10,500 men, and a panzer division had 95 tanks. However, most of the units taking part in the Battle of Berlin were exhausted and weak. Nevertheless, in the beginning of May, Hitler ordered the formation of Army Group Vistula, which was named after a river hundreds of kilometers away at the old border between Germany and Poland. This highest formation was comprised of the 3rd Panzer Army under General Hasso von Manteuffel (considered the best panzer general after Guderian and Rommel; he had commanded the elite

'Grossdeutschland' division) and the 9th Army, which was under the rough, but capable, General Theodor Busse. General Gotthard Heinrici (a very capable officer with great experience in the Eastern Front) was Commander-in-Chief of Army Group Vistula.

Army Group Center was south of Army Group Vistula. It defended the approaches to southern Germany and Bavaria and was under the command of Hitler's favorite general, Field Marshal Ferdinand Schörner, a tough officer, who was not, however, endowed with strategic perception.

The 12th Army (General Walter Wenck) was positioned in the area of the Elbe River, opposite the American vanguards. It was 55,000-men strong and was comprised of the remnants of various units. This Army was Hitler's last hope to save Berlin. The Führer ordered the 12th Army to rush and reinforce the Third Reich's capital, during the Battle of Berlin, but it was impossible for it to reach Berlin before 2 May 1945, when the battle was already concluded.

## Army Group Vistula

Army Group Vistula numbered 482,000 men, who were supported by 700 tanks and self-propelled guns and was comprised of the 3rd Panzer Army and the 9th Army. Its mission was to defend the Oder River line from the Baltic to its confluence with the Neisse River, a distance of 300 kilometers. As the Germans were preparing for their last fight, 18 German divisions - the elite 'Grossdeutschland' Panzer Grenadier Division among them - had been trapped by the Soviets in Courland, in the Baltic region, and were fighting for their survival.

Army Group Vistula's order of battle was the following:

# III SS Germanic Panzer Corps

Under the most capable SS Lieutenant General Felix Steiner commanded four divisions (two panzergrenadier and two grenadier) and other units, some of them later allocated to the 9th Army.

The 11th SS Volunteer Panzer Grenadier Division 'Nordland' *(11. SS-Freiwilligen-Panzergrenadier-Division)*, composed of Danish and Norwegian volunteers, with two panzer grenadier regiments and the 11th SS Panzer Battalion 'Hermann von Salza' *(SS-Panzerabteilung 11. 'Hermann von Salza')*. Its strength was only 5,000 men, 25 tanks and about the same number of armoured vehicles. Its troops fought to the very end, defending the districts of Charlottenburg and Neukölln, as well as the airfield of Tempelhof. Its commanding officer was SS Major General Dr Gustav Krukenberg.

The 23rd SS Volunteer Panzer Grenadier Division 'Nederland.' It was commanded by the SS Major General Jürgen Wagner and was composed of two reduced strength panzer grenadier regiments. It fought to the death in the area of Fürstenwalde, Berlin.

Elements of the 27th SS Volunteer Grenadier Division 'Langemarck' *(27. SS-Freiwilligen-Grenadier-Division Langemarck)* under SS Brigadier Thomas Muller.

Elements of the 28th SS Volunteer Grenadier Division 'Wallonien.'

This corps also fielded six police battalions from the 36th SS Grenadier Division *(Waffen-Grenadier-Division der SS)*, a unit under SS Lieutenant General Dr. Oskar Dirlewanger, which was notorious for its brutality and the 7th Panzer Division *(Panzer-Division)*, composed of 5,000 Luftwaffe pilots turned 'grenadiers,' with no panzers at all. The 3rd Naval Infantry Division *(3. Marine-Infanterie-Division)*, of the German Navy, was also assigned to the 3rd SS Panzer Corps. Its troops had nothing but their personal weapons, some MG 42 machine guns and a number of 'anti-tank fists' *(Panzerfaust)*. The German naval infantry had no training for ground operations. This corps was positioned in the area of the forest of Eberwalde, to the south of the 3rd Panzer Army.

# 3rd Panzer Army

This force was under General Hasso von Manteuffel and was positioned along a 170-kilometer-front, from north of Stettin to the Hohenzollern Canal, 50 kilometers northeast of Berlin. This army was going to face the Soviet forces of the 2nd Belorussian Front, under Field Marshal Konstantin Rokossovsky.

The 3rd Panzer Army fielded the following formations:

● XLVI Panzer Corps *(Panzerkorps)* under General Martin Gareis, with 150 tanks, most of the Panzer IV type. There were also some Panther and some heavy Tiger I tanks.
● The 'Swinemünde' Corps (Lieutenant General John Ansat).

*Inhabitants of Berlin escaping the city at the end of April 1945.*

*One of the Reichstag defenders after the German surrender of 2 May 1945. Out of a total of 5,100 troops that fought for its defense, 2,500 were killed.*

- XXXII Corps (Lieutenant General Friedrich-August Schack).
- Oder Corps (SS Lieutenant General Erich von dem Bach-Zelewski/General Walter Hörnlein).

## 9th Army

The 9th Army was under 47-year-old Lieutenant General Theodor Busse. It had a total of 200,000 men (only 40,000 of them survived), 550 tanks, 700 guns and 600 anti-aircraft guns, which were used in the ground role. Its mission was to bear the brunt of Field Marshal Zhukov's forces and to cover its flanks from Field Marshal Ivan Konev's 1st Ukrainian Front. In addition, it was responsible for the defense of the central sector of the front in the Oder River and the Seelow Heights, the last natural barrier before Berlin.

The 9th Army's order of battle:
- CI Corps
- 25th Panzer Grenadier Division, of almost full strength, with high morale and 75 tanks.
- 4th SS Police Panzer Grenadier Division (*4. SS-Polizei-Panzergrenadier-Division*), commanded by SS Colonel Walter Harzer. It was of reduced strength and its troops carried their personal weapons only.
- LVI Panzer Corps. Its commanding officer, General Helmuth Weidling, was the last commandant of the city of Berlin and the one to order the ceasefire of the Berlin garrison on 3 May 1945. This corps comprised of the 9th Paratroopers Division (*9. Fallschirmjäger-Division*), numbering 20,000 men of administration and supply units with no combat experience at all, the 20th Panzer Grenadier Division (a full strength unit with 65 tanks), the 18th Panzer Grenadier Division with 35 tanks and the Panzer Division 'Müncheberg' (a low strength unit with 30 tanks).
- The Russian Liberation Army (ROA) with 30,000 Russian and Ukrainian nationalists, under the former Soviet General Andrey Andreyevich Vlasov. This was a unit of doubtful fighting value, but its troops fought with the strength of despair.
- Hitler Youth units, aged 10 to 14. General Gotthard Heinrici was infuriated and ordered most of the boys to return to their homes!
- 11th SS Panzer Corps. 'Divisions' with names such as 'Kurmark,' 'Berlin' and 'Döberitz' and others were in its order of battle. Although composed of remnants of other units, they fought courageously.
- Ten battalions of the Volkssturm, with men aged 45 to 70 and armed with panzerfaust and Italian rifles.
- 'Grossdeutschland' Artillery Regiment (*Artillerie-Regiment*).
- 15th SS Grenadier Division elements (*15. Waffen-Grenadierdivision der SS*), composed of Latvians and commanded by SS Major General Karl Burk.
- 32nd SS Volunteer Grenadier Division '30 Januar' elements (*32. SS-Freiwilligen-Grenadier-Division '30. Januar'*). Its troops were students

and teachers of SS officers' training schools. They fought in the southern suburbs of Berlin and few came out of it alive.

● Some 1,150 men from the 33rd SS Grenadier Division 'Charlemagne' *(33. Waffen-Grenadier-Division der SS 'Charlemagne')*. These were French volunteers, commanded by the SS Major Henri Joseph Fenet. Some managed to escape from the Soviets after a titanic fight and joined General Wenck's forces. Finally, they reached the Elbe River and surrendered to the American forces.

# Army Group Center

This army group fielded 700,000 men and was commanded by the fanatical national socialist Field Marshal Ferdinand Schörner. It was arrayed south of Berlin on the approaches to southern Germany and Bavaria and its only formation which took part in the Battle of Berlin was the 4th Panzer Army, which fought against part of Konev's forces. After the ceasefire, Schörner's troops were jailed in Soviet prisoners-of-war camps and very few of them came out alive.

# 12th Army

This force, positioned in the area of the Elbe River, under General Walter Wenck, had 55,000 men, seven self-propelled guns and 40 *Kübelwagens*.

Its troops were from panzer and infantry officers' schools, from the 11th Army and *Volkssturm* units. The formations of the 12th Army were named 'Scharnhorst,' 'Potsdam,' 'Clausewitz' and 'Ulrich von Hutten.' The German military police collected 45,000 stragglers and so the Army reached a strength of 100,000 men. In the beginning of May, and displaying superhuman effort, they

managed to cut through the Soviet lines and joined surviving elements of the 9th Army. Finally, the 12th Army troops surrendered to the American forces in the area of the Elba River.

# Berlin garrison

The Berlin garrison was under the command of Lieutenant General Hellmuth Reymann and comprised of 33,000 policemen, 28,000 over-aged *Volkssturm* troops and 14,000 Hitler Youth members aged 10 to 15. Their armament consisted of *panzerfaust* nd Italian, German, Czech, and British rifles.

Hitler Youth children fought with fanaticism and managed to cause great damage to the Soviet forces, suffering great casualties themselves. On the other hand, many of the over-aged *Volkssturm* members dropped their weapons and headed home. The Berlin garrison was strengthened by SS foreign volunteers, who were forced to move to the town after the 9th Army frontline was breached.

# German forces' morale

Most of the German troops and civilians fought desperately, trying to save Berlin from the 'hordes of Mongolian conquerors.' Many knew in advance that they were doomed; nevertheless, they fought for their motherland. The foreign volunteers fought with courage, defending their ideology as new crusaders, this time against Bolshevism. Others yet fought hoping the British and the Americans would intervene by capturing Berlin first. They could not have known that the decisions for the distribution of zones of influence had already been made by the Allies in the Yalta Conference in Crimea in the beginning of 1945.

# The Battle of Berlin

## The collapse of the 'Thousand-Year' Reich (1945)

Hitler and the other leading personalities of the Third Reich had no doubt that the Battle of Berlin would be the culmination of World War II, after the dramatic turn of the war, due to the consecutive German failures on all fronts. Goebbels used to quote Karl Marx, who said that "whoever possesses Berlin, possesses all of Germany and whoever controls Germany, controls Europe." Stalin ordered the Red Army to capture the capital of the Third Reich in the spring of 1945, using its entire and colossal force, in order to gain the maximum possible political advantages from this victory and establish himself once and for all in the heart of the European continent. The ensuing battle would be so catastrophic, that it is often compared to the most barbaric medieval sieges.

*The last men of the 503rd SS Heavy Tank Battalion along with Panzer Division 'Müncheberg' units defending the PotsdamerPlatz against the Soviet attacks. 'The Last Battle, Berlin, 30th April 1945.' (by David Pentland, published by permission of Cranston Fine Arts - www.davidpentland.com)*

*Beginning on 22 March 1945, General Gotthard Heinrici was, on the one hand, in command of Army Group Vistula and, on the other, was tasked with the unfeasible mission of defending the approaches to Berlin from the incredible force of the Red Army. When the Russians first breached the Oder front, Hitler put all responsibility on Heinrici calling him: "exhausted, indecisive, pedantic, not having the necessary enthusiasm about his job." The reason for this was that Heinrici did not have any qualms about disobeying orders in order to save the lives of his men. His subordinates admired him, considered him "the perfect model of a traditional Prussian officer" and commented positively on the fact that he was unkemptly dressed and preferred the field coat and the World War I leather gaiters to the elegant uniform of the General Staff.*

Field Marshals Georgy Zhukov and Ivan Konev, two of the most eminent military personalities that rose to prominence in the USSR during its titanic fight against Germany, went into Joseph Stalin's great office, in the Moscow Kremlin, on 1 April 1945. They had been called to take part in an important meeting, where Stalin, as well as other highest officers of the State Defense Committee, including General Aleksei Antonov, the stand-in for the Chief of the General Staff, and General Sergei Stemenko, the Head of the Operations Directorate of the General Headquarters Staff *(Stavka)*, would be present. The subject of this meeting was the operation against Berlin, the capital of the hated Third Reich which had caused bloodshed in all of Europe for five and a half years. The two highest officers were in command of the 1st Belorussian and the 1st Ukrainian Fronts respectively and were the main battering ram of the Red Army (thanks to their strength, their operational areas and the courage of their commanders), which was opening its way towards Central Europe.

These two Fronts had already completed the conquest of Pomerania and Upper Silesia and were ready to offer Stalin the much-desired prize of Berlin, towards which the Western Allies' armies were dangerously approaching, passing through the Central German plains. The surprise American advance had aroused suspicions in the Kremlin, which was terrified at the idea of losing the race for Berlin, although it kept pressing the Western Allies for years to open a second front in Europe. After going over the strategic situation and pointing to the rapid Anglo-American advance from the west that, apparently, met no serious resistance,

*Five-and-a-half years of war, the level of responsibilities as Führer, and the murder attempt against him had turned Adolf Hitler into a ghost of himself. As a result, in the spring of 1945, his public appearances were drastically limited. Beevor writes that he "had lost his incredible capacity of memorizing details and statistics with which he used to fight off those who disputed him... and he was no longer interested in stirring up disputes among his colleagues. The only thing he used to notice around him was treason." He decided to stay and die in Berlin on 22 April, sickened by what he considered as treason from his generals and his closest colleagues.*

*During the famous Yalta Conference in February 1945, Churchill, Roosevelt, and Stalin confirmed their will not to accept anything less than Germany's unconditional surrender and set the postwar occupation zones, 'assigning' Berlin's capture to the Red Army.*

Stalin theatrically asked: "Well then, who is going to take Berlin: are we or the Allies?" Konev replied at once: "It is we who will be taking Berlin, and we shall take it before the Allies." It is still a mystery if Stalin feared an allied move towards the German capital or if he just wanted to arouse the competitive mood of his two best field marshals. Moreover, the occupation zones of post-war Germany had been clearly defined in the Yalta Conference and the Soviets had no reason to suspect that the Allies would breach the agreement.

"And how will you be able to organize forces for it: your main forces are at your southern flank, and you'll apparently have to do a good deal of regrouping," Stalin remarked to Konev. Konev replied, with his typical absolute confidence: "You needn't worry, Comrade Stalin. The front will carry out all the necessary measures... ." After analyzing the information on the firepower of the German forces covering Berlin from the estimates they had (Stalin interjected at that moment: "I believe it will be a good battle," listening to the numbers given by Zhukov), Antonov asked how the inter-front boundary between the two powerful Fronts would be drawn on

the map. Stalin grasped the chance to show, for another time, his talent in the politics of "divide and rule." He wanted to finish the war as soon as possible with the fall of Berlin and avoided clearly defining which of the two Fronts would undertake the assault onto the city, though Zhukov's was closer, and, taking advantage of the competition between the two outstanding field marshals, Stalin amended the map showing the plan of the operation, crossing out the part of the demarcation line that cut off the Ukrainian Front from Berlin, allowing it to go as far as Lübben, 60 kilometers southeast of the capital, and no urther. Beyond that line all prospects were open and even the troops of the 1st Ukrainian Front, who would start their assault more to the south would be able to lay claim on the glory of capturing Berlin on equal terms with their colleagues of the 1st Belorussian Front. "Let the one who is first to break in take Berlin," Stalin declared, faithful to the dictators' invariable tactic of "cutting down" military leaders that gather too many military laurels. Stalin, then, asked when the new attack could start and Zhukov and Konev requested two days to study it. After isolating themselves with their staffs and working intensively on it, they replied, on 3 April, that they would be ready to strike on the 16th of the same month.

# Berlin: Third Reich's last fortress

The practice of besieging towns would seem to belong to some bygone era, before the lightning operations of armored and mechanized columns and the hammering of air fleets came to play the leading role in World War II combat. But on the Eastern Front, Hitler had set the three communist

*Despite the lack of any hope, the German troops, exhausted and disillusioned, continued to fight, loyal to their oath to Hitler.*

metropoleis - Leningrad, Moscow, and Stalingrad - as the basic objectives of the 1941 and 1942 campaigns. The Soviets had managed to immobilize the Wehrmacht at their gates and deal a terrible defeat, from which it could never recover. The German leader hastened to adopt a similar tactic, applying lessons learned out of this experience and obeying an inner, natural aversion to giving ground, when his troops had completely lost the initiative, by designating a large number of towns as 'fortresses' (Calais and Boulogne in the west; Königsberg, Poznan, Memel, Breslau in the east). He expected these towns to slow down the allied counterattack. As large urban centers, all European capitals were ideal places for waging defensive battles, thanks to their complex and convoluted road networks, their tightly packed, solidly constructed buildings, their underground installations, their food and fuel depots, their extensive sewer networks and tunnels, and their underground communications.

Hitler's return to Berlin on 16 January 1945, after the final failure of the counterattack in the Ardennes and the commencement of the large Soviet winter attack in the Vistula, along with his conscious decision not to abandon the Reich's capital from that time onwards set the stage for the last, and, perhaps most cruel, siege of the war, which took place there. "I have to force a decision here or fall fighting," Hitler had declared to two of his trusted secretaries on the eve of his birthday in the Chancellery. Berlin was a tough buttress, on which one could support and defend oneself against a numerically superior enemy. In addition, it was different from the other German cities of its era, not only thanks to its size, but also due to its modern character and excellent town planning. It is no coincidence that the Reich capital had endured the hammering from the air admirably and had never faced the danger of extensive destruction, whereas Hamburg, built around the Elbe River estuary, was completely incinerated in

*Hitler showing something on the map to General Theodor Busse, the 9th Army Commander in the Oder front, during a conference in March 1945. First on the left, standing, is Air Force General Ritter von Greim.*

Allied air attacks in July 1943, and historic and elegant Dresden was consumed by fire during a single air raid in February 1945.

In the beginning of World War II, Berlin had a population of 4,300,000 people and was the third largest city in the world. Its residential area consisted mostly of 19th and 20th century apartment buildings, built on solid and deep cellars. Its wide roads and avenues were an effective fire belt, preventing the uncontrolled spread of fires. It had been spared the firestorms that had wiped out other German towns and its civil defense services still functioned properly at that late stage of the war. But Berlin had already lost 25% of its buildings to the massive and merciless blows of the RAF and USAAF. By 21 March 1945, 314 Allied air raids had heaped up a billion cubic meters of ruins in the city, whose population had shrunk to 2.9 million. The destruction of thousands of homes had forced many of its residents to seek shelter in the countryside, but the heaps of rubble left behind made excellent fortified

obstructions, similar to the intact buildings.

The heart of the city pulsed with the spirit of national socialist resistance. Hitler's bunker had been built beneath the Reich Chancellery at the end of 1944 and was practically an extension of a smaller air raid shelter that had first been built in 1936. Its 20 small rooms, at a depth of 17 meters below the Chancellery gardens, included air-conditioned bedrooms and conference rooms, well-equipped storerooms, one kitchen, and independent drinking water and electricity supply systems. Hitler's last headquarters communicated with the outside world through a telephone exchange and a radio. The Chancellery bunker was a perfectly equipped and a self-sufficient complex, 130 stairs below street level, for those who could stand living like troglodytes for a long time.

It is strange that neither the Berliners nor the Allied intelligence services suspected that the German leader was actually in the capital. All believed that he was at Berchtesgaden

## HITLERJUGEND (*HITLER YOUTH COMBAT VOLUNTEER*)

*In the final stages of the war a large number of HJ Volunteers tried to defend their homeland. Some were drafted into the Wehrmacht or attached to Volkssturm units or they fought with their own Hitlerjugend Battalions. Where it was possible they had proper military uniforms and equipment. He wears a black HJ winter uniform. Note the HJ badge worn on his cap. In most cases, HJ volunteers were deployed in the infantry or played anti-tank functions. He is armed with an anti-tank weapon, a Panzerfaust 30 Klein and a Karabiner Kar 98 rifle with ammunition pouches. He also carries M1939 egg grenades, stick grenades and a Hitler Youth dagger. It was common in the last days of the war for these units to be short of weapons and equipment but this youth volunteer has managed to acquire a lot of them. (Illustration by Johnny Shumate / Historical Notes-Comments by Stelios Demiras)*

*In 1945, the Soviet soldier was especially brave and determined to take revenge for the atrocities committed by the Germans in his country. His great victory, though, was tarnished by numerous incidents of inhuman behavior against the German non-combatants.*

where he was organizing his famous 'Alpine Fortress,' ready to continue the fight to the very end. Hitler might have spent much of the war time in austere lodgings and underground headquarters, but he longed for the fresh countryside atmosphere. Moreover, his after-meal walks often gave him the chance for his renowned long drawn-out monologues when he expounded on his political vision. But during the last 105 days of his life he was forced to isolate himself inside his bunker, with the exception of two short outings on 25 February and 13 March, when he made his last public propaganda appearances.

Berlin did not have a garrison at that time. German Army formations were stationed at the borders or in the

various front lines throughout the war, except for a time between the fall of France and the beginning of Operation 'Barbarossa.' Territorial Army units stationed in the interior were exclusively recruiting and training reserves. The only significant fighting units in the German capital in April were the Berlin Guard Regiment *(Wach-Regiment)* of nine companies, from which the elite 'Grossdeutschland' Division evolved, and a flak division. Propaganda Minister Joseph Goebbels, who had been posted as Reich's Defense Commissioner for the Greater Berlin Region *(Gau)* ordered, then, the building of fortification works in and around the city. Thousands of malnourished non-combatants, mostly women, were mobilized to expend what little energy they had left digging anti-tank ditches.

Lieutenant General Hellmuth Reymann, former Commanding Officer of the 11th Infantry Division, was posted as Berlin commandant and was driven to despair when he realized that he had to cooperate with Hitler, Goebbels, Himmler's Replacement Army, the Luftwaffe, Army Group Vistula, the SS, and the Hitler Youth, as well as with the local Nazi Party organizations, which practically controlled the newly-recruited *Volkssturm*. The men of the latter organization were not fed by their service, so they had to be fed by their families.

On 28 March 1945 Hitler relieved General Heinz Guderian of his post as chief of the general staff, after an argument and replaced him with General Hans Krebs, former military attaché in Moscow. Krebs was powerless to carry out his duties. While his duties had to do with the conduct of operations in the Eastern Front only, he could not but be

*T-34/85 tanks
advancing headlong
towards Berlin.*

influenced by the rapid deterioration of operations in the west. The German Army was disintegrating, but the struggle continued.

British historian Alan Bullock stresses the fact that Hitler bore no resemblance to the arrogant victor of 1940 during that dramatic period: "Under the influence of the coming catastrophe, all the primitive forces of his original nature (animal hate, revengeful spirit, destructive passion, intentions incompatible with reality) came to the surface with no constraint. His way of expressing himself became ruder, while his explosions of rage exceeded limits allowed. His orders had no connection with logic, given the fact that he was in no position to realize the chaotic situation dominating the isolated battlefields." Hitler lost all sense of objective and sober judgment and began wasting his time and strength on endless monologues after the failure of the much promising counterattack in the Ardennes in the end of December 1944. His staff talked for hours on end about the details of the operations, Hitler alone took decisions that

sometime later he rejected and finally ended up taking imprudent measures with the only result being new, pointless and bloody sacrifices for the German troops.

The maps on the bunker's walls showed 65 German infantry and 12 panzer divisions in the Western Front, when there actually were no more than 20 battle-worthy formations. New divisions were hastily formed by convalescing troops and Hitler Youth members and given pompous names like 'Potsdam,' 'Klausewitz,' 'Scharnhorst' and 'Nibelugen,' but their fighting value was low as they lacked supplies, weapons and, most of all, the enthusiasm of times before. Hitler was condemned into tragic inaction and his sense of having lost initiative made him often lose his self-control and hurl accusations at his generals and denounce the ungratefulness of the human race, as he was confined to the stifling atmosphere of the bunker. During lunches he stressed his presence by saying: "If I cease to exist, Germany will have no Führer any more. I have no heir!"

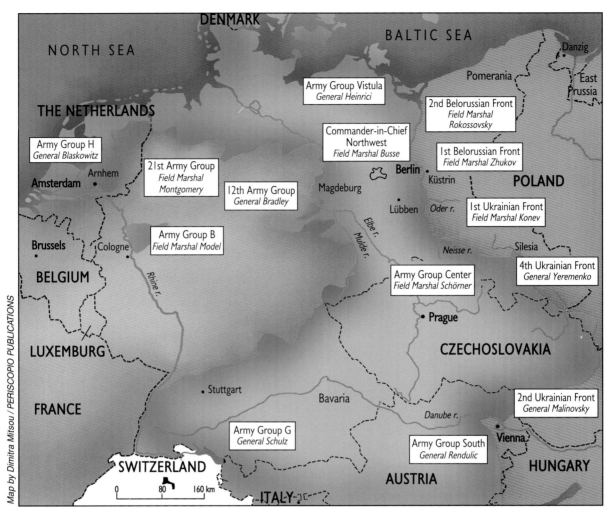

*Map by Dimitra Mitsou / PERISCOPIO PUBLICATIONS*

*The area controlled by the Third Reich had shrunk greatly by 15 April 1945, especially in the direction of Berlin. The powerful forces of the Red Army were preparing to strike and posed an immediate threat to the German capital, once again from the line of the Oder and Neisse Rivers. At the same time, the 'stain' from the British, American, Canadian, and French advance in west Germany was spreading quickly. Berliners, at that time, would say: "The optimists are studying English and the pessimists Russian."*

It is true that Hitler and his associates had been very close to the violence of war they had unleashed. People who had supported him and were 'formed' by him, like Joseph Goebbels, Hermann Göring, Heinrich Himmler, Martin Bormann, and Joachim von Ribbentrop, still had the illusory hope that their leader would find a way to miraculously escape from the tragic situation into which they had fallen. They were competing in lies and machinations, taking great care to silence anyone who suggested that the pointless bloodshed should quickly be brought to an end. Hitler, therefore, was not only immune to common sense, but his belief that

nothing had been lost was boosted, and he imagined that a possible defeat would drag half of humanity into the abyss. "If the war is lost, all the German people will be lost from the face of earth," he had told Albert Speer on 19 March. "The German nation proved to be weak and the future fully belongs to the people of the East. Only the inadequate people survive the struggle. The best men die during the battle."

Indeed, the German leader and the 'Thousand-Year' Reich of which he had dreamed were in an extremely dire situation in the spring of 1945. The V1 and V2 flying bombs had not managed to change the way the war

*VOLKSSTURM* **(PEOPLE'S MILITIA) 1945**
**In 1944 had been formed the German Militia or People's**
**Militia** (*Volkssturm*) **including men 16 to 60 years old.**
**Generally the** *Volkssturmman* **wore no special uniform or**
**clothing; just his regular civilian clothes. But in some cases,**
**military equipment and uniforms were available. On his left**
**arm is the band** *Deutscher Volkssturm Wehrmacht,* **for the**
**members of** *Volkssturm.* **He is holding an anti-tank weapon,**
**a** *Panzerfaust 30.* **The field cap is M1943 type and the overcoat**
**is standard issue of the Army. (Illustration by Johnny Shumate**
**/ Historical Notes - Comments by Stelios Demiras)**

*The 1st Belorussain Front attack in the Seelow Heights was preceded by an artillery barrage that pulverized a great part of the German trenches, crushing those inside, dead or alive. This German soldier was one of the victims. Corpses of soldiers continued to be discovered 50 years later.*

was going, jet aircraft had not gained air superiority, the new and better submarines had no bases from which to operate, the Wehrmacht's counterattacks in Belgium and Hungary had been a resounding failure and Hitler, confined to the cellars of the Chancellery, had clung to the futile hope that a rupture in the Allied coalition would materialize when the Western Allied armies would come into contact with the Soviet ones. In his view, this would save Germany. The section of Foreign Armies East of the Intelligence Department of the Army General Staff had reliable indications that Soviet officers, fearful of a probable American attack, said "we have to saturate the Americans with artillery fire, by mistake, for them to get a taste of the Red Army's whip." US President Franklin D. Roosevelt's death, on 12 April 1945, made Hitler believe that history would be repeat itself and that Germany would be

saved at the last moment (in 1762 Frederick the Great ruled Prussia and the anti-Prussian alliance disintegrated when Empress Elizabeth of Russia suddenly died).

These hopes were unfounded, though. The Allied advance continued steadily and the mighty Third Reich of the past, which had established its iron presence from the Caucasus to the Atlantic and from the North Cape to Cyrenaica, had limited itself to a narrow corridor in central Germany with some pockets to the south in April 1945. Defense in the west was collapsing, but the exhausted Wehrmacht continued fighting with self-sacrifice in the east, out of fear of reprisals for the war crimes it had committed in Russia, or from fear of the Communists and hard labor in Siberia. "Morale is low but discipline rigid," the Soviet intelligence service said. The crushing defeat the Germans had suffered in January and February, when the Red Army liberated Poland in one leap, meant that Germany's resources were exhausted and the country could not wage war for more than a few weeks. The loss of the mines, steel-works and factories of Silesia had afflicted the German war industry more than all the Allied bombings of the Ruhr industrial area over the last two years.

The capital itself was now in danger. Berlin's shield to the east was General Gotthard Heinrici's Army Group Vistula (the name referred to the Germans' vain hopes that they would regain the area around the Vistula River, which they had lost in January). Its total strength was 482,000 men, in addition to its subordinate formations were the 9th Army (General Theodor Busse), which had been badly mauled in western Poland, and the 3rd Panzer Army (General Hasso von Manteuffel.) The

9th Army arrayed four corps: CI Corps in the north, the considerable LVI Panzer Corps (General Helmuth Weidling) in the center of the Seelow Heights with the 20th Panzer Grenadier, the 9th Paratroopers and the newly-formed 'Müncheberg' Panzer Divisions, XI SS Panzer Corps in the south, and V SS Mountain Corps close to the area of Frankfurt an der Oder.

Besides the 25 divisions Heinrici possessed, there was also the Berlin Garrison, a hodgepodge of motley units originating from military schools, paramilitary organizations and training centers. A considerable number of units from the *Volkssturm* (about 50 battalions,) the Hitler Youth, police, air defense services, SS, even 25,000 men from the German Post who had been drafted for military duty, could be added to the divisions. The Army Group Vistula headquarters stated that there were not enough weapons for these untrained men, but the National Socialist authorities insisted on distributing some one-use anti-tank weapons and one hand grenade to each of these men, believing they would drag to death some of the enemy with them. The German capital was also covered by the 4th Panzer Army (Lieutenant General Fritz-Hubert Gräser), which was organic to Army Group Center (Field Marshal Ferdinand Schörner).

The German defense seemed to be sufficient in depth but not manned sufficiently. The three defense lines of the Oder – Neisse line (each 1- to 3-kilometers deep) were fully manned to a depth varying from 20 to 40 kilometers, but the Berlin sector, organized in three concentric defense zones (outer, inner, and center of the city), lacked in personnel and available weapons, perhaps because the German command never believed that the enemy would ever reach the city. For purposes of better control, the defensive ring of the center of the city was subdivided into eight sectors; the one called 'central' included the Reichstag and the Chancellery and was better prepared for protracted defense. All defensive positions were in contact with each other with well protected communication networks, while even the subway was used for concealed transport of reinforcements from sector to sector.

Things were not better in the Oder Front either, and one could see the exhaustion and tension mirrored in the faces of the young recruits. In addition, food rations were reduced from March and the lack of drinking water made many Germans suffer from dysentery. The worst experience, however, was the four-hour night guard duty, when all feared falling into the hands of a Soviet patrol, which would interrogate them in order to get information. Finally, ammunition reserves were so low that their exact number had to be reported daily; each German gun was allowed to fire up to two rounds daily, until the start of the Soviet attack.

*Soviet General Pavel Rybalko, Commanding Officer 3rd Guards Tank Army, was described after the war as the most forceful and capable armor commander of the Red Army.*

Nevertheless, the German troops deeply believed that they had to defend their homeland and families, knowing well that the situation was hopeless. "You cannot believe the terrible hate existing here," wrote a first lieutenant in the Oder line. "I promise you we will sort them out one day. Rapists of women and children will now live through a different kind

*German Jagdtiger
(SdKfz 186) tank
destroyer as it operated
along the banks of the
Rhine River in April
1945. It was one of the
last weapons the Third
Reich produced in its
attempt to stem the tide
of the Allied tanks. It is
finished in a two-color
scheme with Sand
Yellow as the base paint
and irregular stripes of
Dark Green
overpainted. Its 128 mm
KwK 44 L/55 gun on the
elongated hull of
Tiger II was the best the
German military
machine had against the
Allied tanks.
Unfortunately for the
Nazis, these tank
destroyers were
assigned in such few
numbers that they could
do no more than delay
the Reich's end.
(Illustration by Dimitris
Hadoulas / Historical
Notes by Stelios
Demiras)*

of experience. It is not easy to believe what these beasts have done. Each of us has sworn to kill ten Bolsheviks. May God help us in this struggle of ours."

Actually, Hitler believed that the concentration of the Soviet forces in front of Berlin was but a diversion, and that the Red Army attack would first swing against Prague. He estimated that Stalin would rush to occupy the significant Czech industrial area before the Americans got there and that he would give priority to encircling the Bohemian mountains, in order to regain contact with his armies which were laying siege to Vienna. He had told Guderian on the matter: "The Russians are not as foolish as we are. Reaching close to Moscow, when we almost captured the capital, they had stunned us. And look what happened!" So he detached four of the best Waffen SS divisions from Busse and sent them to Schörner in order to cover Czechoslovakia. Hitler's vanity and his refusal to accept reality made him maintain troops, so late in the war, in the cold extremities of northern Norway and caused Germany to have a stronger military presence in Prague than in Berlin.

# The Soviet preparations

During the last weeks of March and the first of April, the 1st Belorussian Front (Field Marshal Georgy Zhukov) and the 1st Ukrainian Front (Field Marshal Ivan Konev) Systematically assembled the forces and supplies they had estimated they would need for their great drive towards Berlin. *Stavka*, leaving nothing to chance, planned the operation with the utmost attention, wanting to avoid a disastrous repetition of the difficulties the Soviet armies had faced in Warsaw in 1920. The Soviet supreme command had overestimated its opponent, believing that at least 90 German divisions would protect Berlin. The Soviets therefore positioned 1,519 tanks and assault guns and 9,303 guns and mortars between Berlin and the Oder and Neisse Rivers. The Soviet command also Feared the possibility of a massive movement of German Army units from the Western to the Eastern Front, although the Anglo-Americans gave them assurances that no such thing had happened.

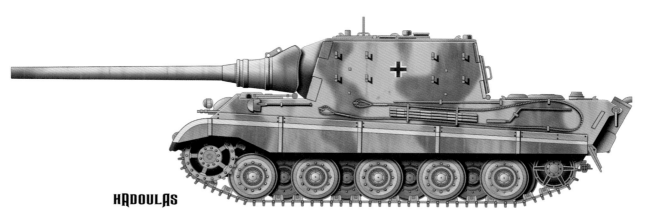

HADOULAS

Experience had shown that a formidable military force, fortified behind a water obstacle, could put up a most determined defense and could check the outnumbering attacking troops. *Stavka's* strategic goals in that last operation were to eliminate the German forces covering the Berlin axis, to capture the city and to attain a smooth link-up with the Western Allies at the Elbe River. While supply services exerted superhuman efforts to collect the war material needed for the coming operation, *Stavka* planned out the operation with cold logic and method. Thus, three Soviet fronts would strike to separate and crush the enemy with converging attacks: the 2nd Belorussian Front (Field Marshal Konstantin Rokossovsky) in the north, the 1st Belorussian Front (Zhukov) in the center and the 1st Ukrainian Front (Konev) in the south. Given the tremendous firepower at its disposal, the Red Army leadership hoped to be able to finish up with the enemy in six days and to occupy Berlin by 22 April, Lenin's birthday anniversary.

Zhukov arrayed seven Soviet armies on the first line (3rd Shock Army, under V. I. Kuznetsov; 5th Shock Army, N. E. Berzarin; 8th Guards Army, V. I. Chuikov; 33rd Army, V.D. Tsvetaev; 47th Army, F. I. Perkhorovich; 61st Army, P. A. Belov; and the 69th Army, V. Ya. Kolpakchi); the 1st Polish Army (S. G. Poplawski), two tank armies (1st Guards Tank Army, under M. Ye. Katukov; and the 2nd Guards Tank Army, S. I. Bogdanov); and four independent manoeuvre corps (2nd and 7th Guards Cavalry Corps, 9th and 11th Tank Corps), while keeping the 3rd Army (A. V. Gorbatov) as reserves. The front would launch its attack from the Küstrin bridgehead with four armies and one corps, supported by 731 tanks and self-propelled guns.

Their mission was to achieve a breakthrough in the formidable German defense lines in the Seelow Heights, gaining at least one breach of sufficient width, through which two tank armies with 1,373 tanks and self-propelled guns would launch and rush to Berlin the next day. Zhukov planned two secondary, supporting attacks: north of Küstrin with the 1st Polish and the 61st Armies and south

*The consecutive defeats that the German Army suffered in the Eastern Front had caused it heavy bleeding. But the veterans who had managed to survive were a formidable opponent for the Soviets in Berlin and this was confirmed by the hundreds of thousands of casualties they caused to the attackers.*

*Soviet assault gun hitting a target in a Berlin building during the first phase of the siege.*

of the bridgehead with the 33rd and 69th Armies and the 2nd Guards Cavalry Corps. In addition, there was something original in this operation: Zhukov planned to attack before dawn, shining 143 searchlights, which were arrayed at a distance of 500 meters between them and the enemy, directly onto the Germans.

Konev, to the left flanks of Zhukov, had four Soviet armies (3rd Guards Army, under V. N. Gordov; 5th Guards Army, A. S. Zhadov; 13th Army, N. P. Pukhov: and the 52nd Army, K. A. Koroteyev), the 2nd Polish Army (K. K. Swierczewski), two tank armies (3rd Guards Tank Army, P. S. Rybalko; and 4th Guards Tank Army, D. D. Lelyushenko) as well as five independent manoeuvre corps (1st Polish, 4th Guards Tank, 25th Tank, 7th Guards Mechanized and 1st Guards Cavalry). The front's attack was more complicated, as the 1st Ukrainian Front would first have to establish a bridgehead on the Neisse River and then separate the German

9th Army from the 4th Panzer Army, pushing the mass of the 963 tanks and self-propelled guns of the two tank armies towards the Spree River and more to the west, towards Brandenburg and Dessau, with the final goal of meeting the Americans on the Elbe River. At the same time, Konev would cover his southern flanks with a secondary strike towards resden and the 28th Army (A. A. Luchinsky) would, later, be detached from the 3rd Belorussian Front and assigned to him, as it would not be able to reach Neisse River by 16 April. Once more, Stalin had Rokossovsky in a supporting role, with five armies and five independent corps to prevent the 3rd Panzer Army from helping Berlin's defence.

Despite the emphasis put on deception, the Red Army could not have hoped to conceal the great attack it planned to launch. The total of the Soviet forces engaged in the operation was 2,500,000 men and women, 6,300 tanks and self-propelled guns, 41,600

*Heavy Soviet tanks advancing towards Berlin through a wooded area. The ground between the Oder and the city was favorable to the defense and slowed down the 1st Belorussian Front's advance.*

guns, rocket launchers and high caliber mortars, and 8,400 aircraft. "It was as if a huge coiled spring was going to shoot up," Captain Vladimir Gal wrote those days. The most fertile imagination could not grasp how much calculation was necessary in order to organize and execute such a colossal attack in such a short time. A total of 29 Soviet armies had to regroup, 15 of which had to cover distances of up to 385 kilometers to reach their launch positions, whereas another three had to cover distances between 300 and 530 kilometers. All the while, Poland's dilapidated railroad network had been burdened with the transport of huge quantities of fuel and ammunition. The 1st Belorussian Front had 7,147,000 rounds of ammunition reserves and arrayed its guns to a density of 295 tubes per square kilometer in the sectors to be breached. Konev had to establish bridgeheads on the left bank of the Neisse River before moving to Berlin and he was assigned 120 engineer battalions and 13 bridging battalions. What is amazing is that all these movements were completed within 15 days, while the preparations for the battles in Belorussia and Vistula – Oder had taken 22 and 48 days respectively.

Additionally, the Soviet field marshals took care to 'clear' a 24-kilometers deep zone of noncombatants, at the rear of their fronts, so as to keep their preparations as secret as possible. The Soviets also had problems with the mass of new recruits that had reinforced first line units. Many of them reached the front having received no more than one week of basic training, while incidents of desertion, insubordination and self-inflicted injuries multiplied. There were others who yearned for glory and were looking forward to adding a medal from the Battle of Berlin to their collection. Others, yet, more practical minds, became members of the Communist Party, so that their families would be notified if they fell during the battle.

While Stalin and the *Stavka* deluded themselves by believing that, with a bit of luck, they would be able to capture Berlin by 22 April, the greatest majority of the plain Soviet troops did not consider leading this great operation as such an honor as Zhukov and Konev would have hoped. Most were veterans of many years of a tough war

*Soviet B-4 203 mm howitzer hammering the German positions west of the Oder River. Field Marshal Konev did not hesitate in admitting that the Red Army "hadn't faced a lack of artillery rounds for years," using them lavishly.*

*General Helmuth Weidling (first left) commander of the Berlin Defense Area.*

and, now that victory seemed close, the longing for their close relatives and the wish to survive and return safe and sound was growing stronger and stronger. They felt lonely, and this feeling was worsened by the fact that they were hundreds of kilometers away from their home and they could not even listen to the Russian radio. Nevertheless, these men wanted to return home with a medal at any cost. The casualties they had sustained until then deprived the Red Army of many of its cadres; however, the ones who survived had solid war experience and high morale, fed by the excitement for the coming victory and a strong desire for revenge. The daily order Zhukov issued to his troops mentioned: "Soviet soldier, take revenge! Behave in such a way that not only today's Germans, but their descendants far in the future, will tremble when they remember you. Everything that belongs to the Germans is yours. Soviet soldier, shut your heart to all feelings of mercy!"

## All fronts collapse

National Socialist Germany was being crushed in the vice formed by the Allied and Soviet armies, relentlessly advancing deeper and

deeper into the heart of Europe, as Zhukov and Konev prepared frantically for the titanic battle for the enemy capital. The 3rd and 4th Ukrainian Fronts troops attempted a daring leap along the Danube valley on 1 April 1945 and in a week's time were fighting in the suburbs of Vienna, which fell on 13 April. The large towns of the Reich were captured one after another under the combined blows of seven Allied armies: 1st Canadian, 2nd British, 1st, 3rd, 7th and 9th American and 1st French. Thanks to a rare stroke of luck, General Dwight Eisenhower's plan for a careful attack on the dangerous line of the Rhine River was not implemented, since the fast American vanguards captured the Remagen Bridge intact on 7 March and secured a valuable bridgehead on the eastern banks of the river at no cost. On 10 March Hitler relieved the old Field Marshal Gerd von Rundstedt from his duties as Commander in Chief West, replacing him with Albert Kesselring, but it was impossible to check the gap. The Allied forces smashed through this breach and managed to completely surround 325,000 German soldiers in the huge Ruhr Pocket by 1 April, leading the tough Field Marshal Walter Model to commit suicide 17 days later, as he did not want to follow his men into surrender.

The American troops reached the western banks of the Elbe River on 11 April, after another offensive leap. This river had already been fixed in 1944 as the dividing line between the western and the Soviet occupation zones in post-war Germany. The troops of the 38th Infantry Division thought they would continue moving towards Berlin, which was only 110 kilometers away, but Eisenhower was in no mood to sacrifice 100,000 of his

*SS-SCHARFÜHRER (**SERGEANT**)*
**Of special note are the Waffen-SS camouflage
smock and helmet cover of the M1942 type and
here in the so-called 'plane tree' pattern, with
the autumn/winter side exposed. He wears the
standard-issue field gray service dress trousers
and marching boots. He is armed with an
MP 40 machine pistol with two triple canvas
magazine pouches. He carries a bread bag,
water bottle, bayonet, and gasmask. The
MP 40** *Schmeisser* **was a classic German Army
and Waffen-SS weapon. Note the unfolded
stock of the gun. The MP 40 replaced the
MP 38 as the standard submachine gun. The
MP 40 became synonymous with the German
Army. (Illustration by Johnny Shumate /
Historical Notes-Comments by Stelios Demiras)**

*Lieutenant General Walter Wenck played a decisive, though indirect, role in the Battle of Berlin as the 12th Army commander.*

# Zhukov is late and Konev advances

The two fronts launched their attacks on 16 April 1945. The artillery barrage in the 1st Belorussian Front's sector began at 0500 and lasted only 30 minutes, but was, nevertheless, extremely intense. It was so fierce that it could be heard in the southeastern suburbs of Berlin, 60 kilometers away, like a small-scale earthquake. "The houses trembled," Beevor writes, "pictures fell from the walls and the phones were ringing." Not surprisingly, this terrible artillery barrage created more obstacles for the attackers, such as craters and ruins, than the ones it destroyed. The ground had been so dug up from the bombardment, that the Soviet anti-tank guns and the divisional artillery could not follow the infantry. In addition, the German second line of defense in the Seelow Heights remained almost intact, and the soft ground did not allow the endless Soviet columns to move off road, resulting in an unbelievable traffic jam.

men (this is the number of casualties for the capture of Berlin that his staff estimated), a city that would have then to be given to Stalin, according to the agreements signed. Therefore, he preferred remaining idle at the Elbe, waiting for the Red Army. At the same time, the British and the Canadians were in the north, consolidating Germany's coast and the French completed the occupation of Bavaria in the south. The only ones responsible for Berlin were the Russians.

To make matters worse, the capture of Berlin was not just another operation, like the ones during the Great Patriotic War, but a race between two most capable colleagues and competitors. In November 1944, Stalin had promised Zhukov that he would be privileged to capture the Reich's capital (Zhukov had been the Soviet dictator's personal military adviser and the architect of the great victories of the past). Things, however, took a different direction after the decisive conference of 1 April in Moscow.

The honorary vanguard could not have been any other than Vasily Chuikov's 8th Guards Army, the veterans of the Battle of Stalingrad. Its troops had sworn to fight without any thoughts of falling back and big pieces of cardboard in the shape of keys had been distributed to them to remind them of the keys of Berlin that had been given to the Russians in 1760. The German defense in the Seelow Heights was so stubborn and decisive, though, that the Soviet troops advanced very little until the end of the day, despite the constant support offered by tanks and self-propelled guns, while the 69th Army to the south was pinned down. The

*Soviet Il-2 Shturmovik ground attack aircraft flying over Berlin on 30 April 1945. The aircraft in the foreground carries the slogan 'Avenger' on its fuselage.*

Frankfurt garrison repulsed all attacks, the V SS Mountain Corps kept its positions on the Oder and the XI SS Panzer and the CI Corps yielded not an inch to the enemy. Clearing the German minefields proved to be more complex than had been planned and casualties from mines were excessively large.

Results were discouraging, despite the hundreds of thousands of rounds that had been fired against the Germans and the Red Air Force's 6,500 sorties over the Seelow Heights. Zhukov's idea to use searchlights worked against his troops, as their blinding beams of light reflected on the smoke and dust, disorientating the attackers. In addition, air reconnaissance wasn't able to show that the ground morphology of the Seelow Heights, overlooking the Soviet bridgehead, was worse than Zhukov believed. The experienced Army Group Vistula commander, General Heinrici, realized the extent of the storm that was to fall on his positions and had retired most of the frontline units to the second line on the previous day. Thus, the 1st Belorussian Front's hammer fell flat.

Watching it from an advanced observation post, Zhukov realized that his attack was disappointing, which

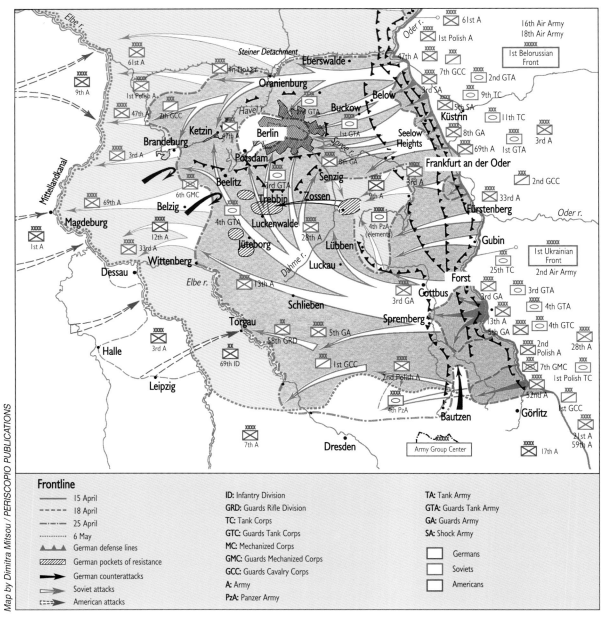

### Frontline

| | |
|---|---|
| —— | 15 April |
| – – – | 18 April |
| –·–·– | 25 April |
| ········ | 6 May |
| ▲▲▲ | German defense lines |
| ▨▨▨ | German pockets of resistance |
| ➤ | German counterattacks |
| ⟹ | Soviet attacks |
| ⟾ | American attacks |

**ID:** Infantry Division
**GRD:** Guards Rifle Division
**TC:** Tank Corps
**GTC:** Guards Tank Corps
**MC:** Mechanized Corps
**GMC:** Guards Mechanized Corps
**GCC:** Guards Cavalry Corps
**A:** Army
**PzA:** Panzer Army

**TA:** Tank Army
**GTA:** Guards Tank Army
**GA:** Guards Army
**SA:** Shock Army

☐ Germans
☐ Soviets
☐ Americans

Map by Dimitra Mitsou / PERISCOPIO PUBLICATIONS

*Using a wide outflanking maneuver, the 1st Belorussian and the 1st Ukrainian Fronts smashed the German defense west of the Oder and Neisse Rivers, broke up the 9th Army and the 4th Panzer Army sectors and completely encircled Berlin.*

infuriated him. Making the same error that had troubled the Soviet command and caused the failures of 1942, he decided to engage his armored reserves at once, in order to achieve a breakthrough, instead of keeping them for the exploitation phase. When the 1st and 2nd Guards Tank Armies moved slowly forward, they tried to do so through the thick mud and were immobilized in the traffic chaos that in which the mechanized units and the guns of the other armies, had already become entangled. The situation only grew worse. The 11th Tank Corps (1st Guards Tank Army) repulsed a weak counterattack launched by the 'Müncheberg' Panzer Division with ease, but the two Soviet tank armies failed to use their firepower to the maximum effect. Each time they tried to move through the fortified German

***GERMAN MACHINE GUNNER***
*Of special note are the Waffen-SS camouflage smock, trousers and helmet cover in the so-called 'herringbone twill M44' dot camouflage, autumn/winter side exposed. He wears lace up boots and canvas gaiters. The MG 42 general purpose machine gun 7.92 mm was extremely reliable, highly resistant to dust and cold conditions and was very popular in the German Army. It was first used in action at Ghazala in May 1942 and more than 750,000 MG 42s were made before the war ended. (Illustration by Johnny Shumate / Historical - Notes Comments by Stelios Demiras)*

*Despite the heroism displayed by many of the defenders of Berlin, some of the German soldiers preferred to give themselves up to the Soviets when they reached the limits of their endurance and realized that there was no hope.*

villages, they were attacked by a volley of rockets from panzerfausts, and at a very short distance at that, which made them even more lethal.

Faced with the prospect of a resounding failure, Zhukov lost his temper with his subordinate commanders and demanded that they all personally lead their units, carrying out their duties from the front line. Officers deemed "incapable of fulfilling the missions assigned to them" or the ones showing "lack of determination" were threatened to be relieved on the spot. "Tanks and infantry cannot expect artillery to kill all Germans," the field marshal said in his orders. "Do not show mercy. Keep on moving day and night." The tactics of threatening first and then encouraging, so fitting to the forceful and extremely demanding Zhukov, brought results immediately. The advance rate increased, though the 1st Belorussian Front had to fight a tough battle for two entire days in order to

capture the Seelow Heights so that it could achieve a rudimentary freedom of movement. The right flank of the German 9th Army continued to cling to the Oder riverbank, but the left flank was forced back under terrible pressure. A large number of tanks rushed from the two breaches at Müncheberg and Briesen, though Busse continued sending reports about the heroic defense of his units, which had destroyed another 82 Soviet tanks in a few hours. The 1st Guards Tank Army was unlucky enough to have to face the *Königstiger* tanks of the 502nd SS Heavy Tank Battalion *(schwere SS-Panzer-Abteilung 502)*.

Zhukov's egoism cost his men dearly. The Soviet troops lying dead in front of the German positions in the Seelow Heights were piling up and they remained there for days before being buried, creating the danger of epidemics. The wounded were often left where they fell in the battlefield for up to 20 hours until the medical units collected them. Amid the chaos, incidents of friendly fire were numerous, and the Soviet command system often collapsed.

Nine German low-strength divisions succeeded in slowing down and seriously wearing out the 8th Guards Army and then fell back easily to the second line of defense. This maneuver was followed by a new, though unsuccessful German counterattack with a force of three divisions on 17 April. The Germans were trying to cut the Berlin-Küstrin highway, directly behind the advancing 1st Guards Tank Army of Lieutenant General Katukov. The next day, Chuikov was forced to storm, at a great expense, the German third line of defense, which Soviet reconnaissance had failed to discover the previous days. Even the most courageous troops could not have lasted a long time under the pressure of the Soviet forces, which were clearly superior in strength and firepower. Thus, the 5th Shock Army and the 8th Guards Army completed the breaching of the third defense line between Buckow and Batzlow on 20 April, and then continued to the eastern suburbs of Belin. Significant German forces, such as the Frankfurt an der Oder garrison numbering 30,000 men, were left behind and were cut off from the main German force.

Throughout the difficult time the 1st Belorussian Front was facing, Stalin did not stop from reproaching Zhukov for underestimating his opponent and urging him, at the same time, to move faster. Zhukov's smaller flank attacks were more successful, however. The 3rd Shock and the 47th Armies had already outflanked Berlin from the north and the 33rd and 69th Armies had cut off the main forces of the German 9th Army from the

capital, opening the way for the ensuing complete encirclement of Busse's forces. At the same time, Rokosovsky's 2nd Belorussian Front, which had launched its own attack in the area of Stettin on 20 April, significantly helped Zhukov's advance by pressing the German defenders of the lower Oder and obstructing the 3rd Panzer Army from helping Busse's badly suffering forces.

Heinrici decided to use part of his reserves and dispatched the III *(Germanic)* SS Panzer Corps, under General Felix Steiner in an attempt to stabilize that sector of the front. The force included the 11th SS Volunteer Panzer Grenadier Division 'Nordland,' the 23rd SS Volunteer Panzer

*Three of the invisible protagonists of the last days of the Third Reich in a 1944 photo: the Commander-in-Chief of the Luftwaffe Field Marshal (Reichsmarschall) Hermann Göring (left), who was denounced by Hitler on the charge of treason, the Chief of the Supreme Command of the Armed Forces (OKH) Field Marshal Wilhelm Keitel, who loyally served his leader to the end and Grand Admiral Karl Dönitz, Commander-in-Chief of the Navy, who was designated by Hitler as his heir.*

*Field Marshal Ivan Konev, Commander-in-Chief 1st Ukrainian Front in 1945.*

*SS General Felix Steiner (1896-1966), was not only trusted by his troops, but was, in fact, adored. However, for objective reasons, he was not in a position to accomplish the mission to save Berlin, assigned to him by Hitler.*

Grenadier Division 'Nederland,' the 27th SS Volunteer Grenadier Division 'Langemarck,' the 28th SS Volunteer Grenadier Division 'Wallonien,' and other units. Heinrici ordered Steiner immediately to collect all men in the Oranienburg area who could fight and deploy them to cover the right flank of Manteuffel's 3rd Panzer Army, which was in danger of collapsing. As for the 9th Army, it started breaking apart and was moving in three different directions, which was what General Busse was afraid of. CI Corps was forced to withdraw towards Eberswalde and the area north of Berlin, LVI Panzer Corps fell back east of Buckow towards the capital and the XI SS Panzer Corps was pushed southwest towards Senzig. The German defense had been cut up, but Steiner and the CI Corps in the north were a potential danger to Kuznetsov's advance with the 3rd Shock Army.

Zhukov, for his part, was confident about the progress of the campaign against the Germans. He was less worried about his northern flanks than about the progress Konev was making in the south, where his rival's forces had approached Zossen and the Spree River. The reconnaissance patrols sent out by the 1st Belorussian Front were more eager to pinpoint the 1st Ukrainian Front positions than the German ones. When Zhukov ordered his advancing army to "penetrate tonight into Berlin without fail," on 20 April, he had already concentrated the massive firepower of the 6th Breakthrough Artillery Division within

range of the German capital and had began blasting its streets with highcaliber rounds. Optimism soared and Red Army political department units erected signs at the sides of the road: "Be terrified fascist Germany! The time to settle up has come!" But when Zhukov's advance slowed in the face of stiff German resistance, the Soviets were lucky that Konev was able to storm rapidly up to the environs of Berlin from the south, proving, for the umpteenth time, that the geometrical rule that "a straight line is the shortest distance between two points" is not valid in the operational art of war. The 1st Ukrainian Front launched its drive towards Berlin with a terrible, 145-minute artillery barrage against enemy, that was extremely successful, thanks to the thorough reconnaissance that had pinpointed targets earlier. The lethal and continuous artillery fire helped Soviet troops bridge the Neisse River between Forst and Bad Muskau without any delays at 133 points and to get the pontoons ferrying the T-34 tanks almost at once. The 5th Guards and the 13th Armies had already been in contact with the German second defense line by the end of 16 April. A German counterattack launched the next day failed to check Konev and he penetrated another 18 kilometers. In the meantime, the cloudy sky and the rain gave place to better weather conditions, which boosted the advance to full speed.

"Trying to check our advance, the Hitler command committee to action against us in the second and third lines of defence six panzer and five infantry divisions from their reserves," Konev wrote in his memoirs. "Small wonder. We were delivering a blow at their weakest spot, and if they did not foresee a complete catastrophe they had a presentiment of a good deal of trouble... . After desperately trying to stop us in the second line of defence the Germans no longer had adequate forces for the third line of defence on the Spree." The 1st Ukrainian Front had managed to break through all the enemy's defense lines, to isolate Cottbus and Spremberg and to cross the Spree River south of Berlin with both its tank armies by the end of 18 April, supported by 7,517 air force sorties. Rybalko (3rd Guards Tank Army) crossed the river first. He had discovered a shallow fording point in the 50-meter-wide river and when his tanks splashed the river he realized, to his great relief, that the water barely covered their tracks. At the same time, the 52nd and the 2nd Polish Armies continued their advance on the Dresden axis, repulsing a dangerous German counterattack launched from the direction of Görlitz, among others.

Despite the German resistance, the Soviet Army advanced through eastern German territory with a stormy feeling of anger mingled with joy. "Everyone seemed to have a harmonica with him," wrote Vasily Grossman, a war reporter for the Red Army newspaper Krasnaya Zvezda. The harmonica is "the troops' musical instrument par excellence, since it is the only instrument that can be played on a vehicle or a cart as it goes bumping along." While 1st Ukrainian Front troops were advancing at full speed through Schlieben and Luckau, and approaching the *OKH* headquarters at Zossen, their commander received a phone call from Stalin on the night of 17 April. The Soviet dictator believed that Konev was in the ideal position to deal the final blow against Berlin and that the southern approaches had proved to be clearly easier for the Red Army, while the 1st Belorussian Front had to clear its way with great difficulty through the expertly fortified approaches to the east of the city, having to face countless groups armed with *panzerfausts*. Therefore, Stalin suggested assigning Zhukov's two tank armies to him, so he could use them in his own sector, a move that was logistically complex and would result in a lot of lost time. Konev replied that he could threaten Berlin with his own forces, and Stalin agreed to turning the main effort of the operations towards the north: "Very good," he said. "I agree. Turn the tank armies towards Berlin." Zhukov was informed of this change of plans right away. The Kremlin leader's intervention for a change in the axes of attack and his decision for Konev to attack Berlin as well, could create accidents between the two fronts, but, on the other hand, it quickened the rate of advance, thanks to the rekindled competition between the two field marshals.

*German Panzerkampfwagen VI Ausf B (SdKfz 182) Königstiger* **heavy tank, Berlin, April 1945. The remnants of these tanks made a last effort, along with units of Peoples' Grenadiers (Volksgrenadier), to check the Soviet attack on the Chancellery. The 'King Tiger' was armed with a KwK 43 L/71 88 mm gun and two MG 34 7.92 mm machine guns and its armor was up to 180 mm (in its front). The fact that it was only available in small quantities meant that it could not stem the mass of Allied tanks on the Western or the Eastern Front, despite its great firepower. Finished in a three-color scheme with Sand Yellow as the base paint and irregular stripes of Red Primer and Dark Green overpainted. (Illustration by Dimitris Hadoulas / Historical Notes by Stelios Demiras)*

HADOULAS

# "The Russians will be dealt the largest defeat in their history!"

The news of the breakthrough in the Oder Front led most Reich ministers to abandon Berlin, especially once it was obvious that its defense was based on a rabble of scattered units with the *Volkssturm* and the Hitler Youth at their core. Hitler, though, had not been persuaded to leave the capital for Berchtesgaden or another, safer location in the Bavarian Alps. On 17 April he still declared his faith in the final victory, saying that "...the Russians will be dealt the greatest defeat in their History at the gates of Berlin!" On 20 April, his 56th birthday was celebrated with a strange solemnity in the bunker, which the dictator left for a while, in order to inspect an SS unit and to give medals to several Hitler Youth members, orphans of the bombing of Dresden, who were defending Berlin with fervor. This was going to be his last public appearance, but his influence on the German people and the Wehrmacht remained as strong as ever.

The Soviets had a surprise present of their own for Hitler's birthday: the city came into range of the 5th Shock Army's heavy artillery on the same day and the constant lethal storm over it commenced. Rounds fired by the Soviet guns had slogans written on them, such as: "For Stalingrad," "For Ukraine," "For the widows and the orphans," "For the mothers' tears," "For Goebbels the rat." At the same time, an outflanking maneuver aimed at isolating the German capital from the north, as the 2nd Guards Tank Army had captured Bernau, only 16 kilometers northeast of Berlin and continued to Oranienburg, 30 kilometers north of the city. Zhukov's left flank progressed too, as it succeeded in pushing a panzer wedge to the southwest towards Senzig, at the rear of the 9th Army, 32 kilometers east of Berlin.

Mixed units from the 1st Belorussian Front gave their first battles in the city's suburbs on 21 April and began penetrating towards its center. The German command knew that there was no chance of effectively organizing a central command of the scattered rabble that would defend Berlin. Obtaining precise information on the rapidly changing situation was practically impossible and the orders issued from Hitler's bunker usually reached units too late to be implemented. Events had already superseded them. Confusion reigned in the German command. On one occasion, a false rumor that General Weidling had been in the western suburbs of the city, while his LVI Panzer Corps was fighting in the east, lead Hitler to sentence him to death in absentia for desertion.

At that last hour of despair, when Hitler's strategic genius collapsed, there were men who had decided to fight to the end for him and his ideals.

*Berliners in a queue waiting to receive some potable water after the complete destruction of the water supply system by bombings. The National Socialist leadership, although having decided to fight for Berlin, had taken no measures for the evacuation of the noncombatants from the cit – an omission that had tragic consequences.*

The Germans continued fighting passionately as if acting in a strange dream, regardless of their reasons for fighting: patriotism, ideological conviction, coercion by the military police, or fear of the SS 'flying courtmartials' that were hanging deserters on lamp posts with a sign around their necks saying: "I have been hanged because I did not believe in the Führer." Albert Speer, Hitler's favorite architect and the Minister of Armaments, visited the bunker on 23 April but left a few hours later. Others who tried to avoid the Soviet artillery were Foreign Minister Joachim Ribbentrop, his aide Julius Schaub, Admiral Von Puttkamer and Hitler's personal doctor, Dr. Theodor Morell. Others yet took greater risks in order to get to the bunker, like the General of the Air Force Ritter von Greim and renowned pilot Hanna Reitsch, who landed with a light plane a little further from the Chancellery on 26 April.

In the meantime, the Germans were fighting desperately in the suburbs of Berlin to delay an enemy who not only had more troops, but was also well-equipped with a variety of heavy weapons. This heroic struggle made Hitler hope that, perhaps, not everything had been lost yet and that the Wehrmacht could, possibly, repulse the invaders, as the Soviets had done to the Germans at the gates of Moscow in 1941. In one of his last moments of euphoria and decisiveness that had charmed people so much in the past, Hitler declared on 21 April: "Whoever wants can leave! I intend to stay put." Zhukov's tanks entered the northeastern suburbs, close to the

*The conclusion of the Battle of Berlin was written on 24 June 1945 in Moscow's Red Square with the great Red Army Victory Parade. Part of the ceremony involved lowering 200 German standards and banners in front of Lenin's Mausoleum. It was the time of absolute triumph for the USSR.*

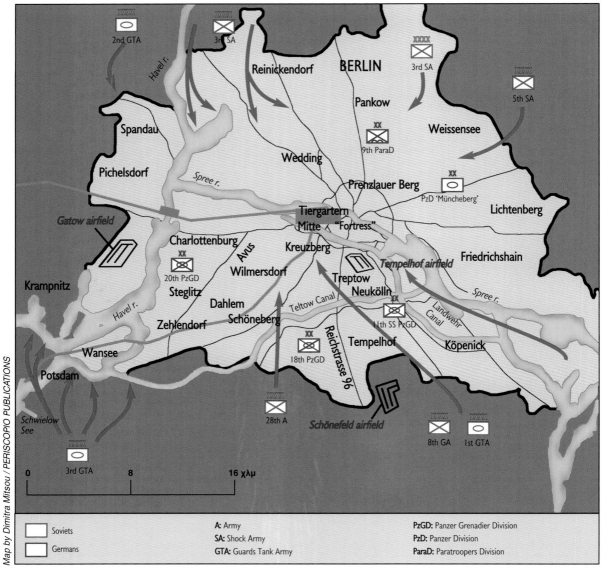

Map by Dimitra Mitsou / PERISCOPIO PUBLICATIONS

**Legend:**

- Soviets
- Germans

**A:** Army
**SA:** Shock Army
**GTA:** Guards Tank Army

**PzGD:** Panzer Grenadier Division
**PzD:** Panzer Division
**ParaD:** Paratroopers Division

*In 1945 the greater Berlin area took up 820 square kilometers wide and was intersected by major water obstacles, such as the Havel River in the west, the Spree in the south and the Landwehr Canal. The Soviets attacked the city from all directions, taking advantage of their overwhelming manpower superiority.*

subway terminals, followed by units appropriately equipped for siege warfare in the morning of the same day. Chuikov's veterans knew the secrets of street-fighting and of close combat in inhabited areas very well and formed assault groups of one rifle company, five or six anti-tank guns, one tank or self-propelled gun platoon, two engineer platoons and one flame-thrower platoon. The basic idea was to use the heavy weapons to crush or burn down the enemy resistance points and then for the

infantry to consolidate the area. At the same time, artillery and rocket fire fell unrelentingly, in salvoes, preparing the next infantry 'leaps' and obliterating the building blocks where the enemy was fortified. Medical units were directly behind the combat troops, ready to intervene since especially heavy casualties are often caused during street fighting, not only from gunfire but also from accidents caused by buildings falling and from the traps hidden in the heaps of rubble.

*SS-ROTTENFÜHRER (**CORPORAL**)*
*He wears reversible parka with the camouflage side for autumn and field gray service dress trousers. Note the lace-up boots and gaiters. He sports a Western Front button-hole ribbon. Note the emblem and the SS rank badge on the collar. He is armed with a Gewehr 43 semi automatic 7.92 mm rifle. The G43 was extensively used on the Eastern Front, being first issued in 1943 but was found in smaller numbers on other fronts. The quality was always to satisfactory standard so the weapon had a good reputation for accuracy and reliability. (Illustration by Johnny Shumate / Historical Notes-Comments by Stelios Demiras)*

*Soviet Field Marshals Zhukov (left) and Rokossovsky had risen to prominence from the lowest echelons of the Red Army thanks to their exceptional capabilities. The troops respected them but feared them as well.*

Konev maneuvered from the south in order, first, to complete the 9th Army's encirclement and then to approach the capital's southern suburbs, while 1st Belorussian Front's troops fought their first deadly street-fighting battles in Berlin. His two tank armies advanced by 40-50 kilometers both on 19 and 20 April, but the field marshal was not satisfied and called the 3rd Guards Tank Army commander on the radio to hurry: "Comrade Rybalko, you move like a tortoise! A single brigade is fighting while the rest of the Army is stuck." Lelyushenko's tanks (4th Guards Tank Army) captured the largest German Army ammunition depot left in the town of Juteborg and reached Luckenwalde, 40 kilometers south of Berlin. Rybalko, advancing on flat ground, crossed Dahme River and approached Zossen, the seat of the German headquarters and the complex telephone and teletype center, thanks to which *OKH* had managed to keep, until then, rudimentary contact with the various German units still

fighting in the shrinking Reich state. Krebs, in desperation, sent a mechanized company of 250 men under First Lieutenant Kränkel against Rybalko, but they could not stop the Soviets from capturing Zossen on 22 April.

Prestige still played a crucial role, however. Zhukov wanted to force Konev to give up his attempt to attack Berlin from the southwest. On 21 April, Zhukov ordered the 8th Guards Army to swing to the south, towards the Spree River, so that it could enter the city together with the 1st Guards Tank Army from the same direction, obstructing Rybalko in the process. At the same time, Zhukov sent the 47th Army towards Spandau on a wide outflanking maneuver and the 2nd Guards Tank Army to Oranienburg. Konev continued coming up from the south and the 5th Mechanized Corps (4th Tank Guards Army), in the southwest of Berlin, repulsed attempts from other German units to approach the city from the southwest. Army Group Center desperately launched powerful counterattacks from the area of Görlitz in the south between 20 and 26 April, in an attempt to re-establish contact with 9th Army remnants.

Heinrici made no attempt to breach the gap opened by the 1st Belorussian Front and, when Krebs pressed him to comply with Hitler's orders and to counterattack at once, he preferred to ignore them. He believed that the 9th Army's only chance was to fall back immediately to the west, which would further widen the gap that was going to seal Berlin's fate. The LVI Panzer Corps commander, General Helmuth Weidling, who was trying to bypass Berlin in the south to occupy new positions close to Potsdam, was ordered to get into the capital and defend it.

*Beginning 21 April 1945, Berlin was being subjected to a daily raid of Soviet artillery rounds, which caused terrible damage and heavy casualties to the non-combatant population.*

The German civilians were expecting the advancing Red Army with mixed feelings of fear, awe and curiosity. The Soviets "were not the conquerors the Germans expected," Beevor comments. "Their worn-out brown uniforms, stained and torn to pieces, their worn-out boots and the pieces of rope on their guns, instead of gun belts, was a completely different breed of victors, compared to the victorious Wehrmacht of times before in the newsreels." Nevertheless, the invader was incredibly strong and indifferent to human casualties, something to which miserable refugee convoys rushing to get away could testify. The roads used by the Soviet mechanized columns rushing at full speed were full of broken carts that the Soviet tanks had thrown into the ditches, looted baggage all around, bed-sheets, cooking utensils, suitcases and toys. German prisoners of war who were moved to the rear stared with awe at the armored, self-propelled gun and other tracked vehicle columns, wondering: "Is this the army that in 1941 was supposed to be in the throes of death?" Soviet soldiers who met them on the other side of the road, jeered at them, saying "Hitler kaput" and accompanying it with the characteristic gesture denoting beheading.

# "Mein Führer, Steiner did not attack"

The Soviet tanks were in the suburbs of Berlin and were fighting in Niederschönhausen and Lichtenberg. Hitler grew more melancholy and had fits of rage against the Germans: "A nation of cowards! It leaves its women to be raped and poison its land. It is put to flight in the East. It surrenders to the enemy in the West. It was not worthy of National Socialism." However, he started planning a new attempt, on 21 April, in order to close the ominous gap in Heinrici's front, northeast of Berlin. The Soviet move of encircling the city from the north left its army's right wing exposed and Hitler believed that he could strike there and crush the enemy. He ordered Steiner's corps, coming from the north, to advance south during the night, moving from Eberswalde to the capital. If Steiner succeeded in his objective, Zhukov's vanguard advancing to Berlin would be cut off and a new triumphant turn of luck would encourage the German Army, prolonging the fighting.

Hitler's hopes depended on Army Detachment Steiner, as this temporary formation was called, and his optimism for what the SS General

*A German instructor training a Hitler Youth member in the use of the* panzerfaust *portable anti-tank launcher, while, it the background, other soldiers wait for their turn.*

could achieve was for all to see, even though Heinrici had limited him to a secondary role. "They had assigned the ridiculous task of covering the flanks to a man like Steiner," Hitler shouted and was sure that the faithful SS troops would once more offer a solution, as they had done many times in the past. The order given to Army Detachment Steiner clearly showed the hysteria reigning in the bunker at that time: "Any commanding officer who keeps men back will forfeit his life within five hours. You will guarantee with your head that absolutely every man is employed." However, more and more German soldiers and young recruits showed signs of unwillingness to die for a lost cause.

Busse, in the meantime, with the largest part of the 9th Army (XI SS Panzer Corps, V SS Mountain Corps and the Frankfurt an der Oder garrison) retreated sideways, southwest, towards Spreewald, despite orders received from Hitler's bunker not to abandon the Oder defense line under any circumstances. The remaining German units were a slow-moving mixture of mutilated divisions and terrified non-combatants who were trying to escape the Red Army. Busse's troops moved through thick pinewoods in small groups and were no longer able to receive orders from their headquarters. When a vehicle broke down or ran out of fuel, they abandoned it on the road and continued on foot. The busy Heinrici, who was trying to save his troops, continued insisting that the 9th Army should withdraw "south of the lakes, southeast of Berlin" and that meant abandoning the capital. He was also

against Steiner's attack and asked to be relieved. Any other time, Hitler would have beheaded him without hesitation, but, at the time, there was a lack of experienced generals and he could not choose a new commander for the Army Group Vistula, so Heinrici remained in his position. The unlucky Berlin Commandant though, Lieutenant General Reymann, was replaced by Colonel Kaethe, a staunch Nazi.

It is not known what orders Heinrici gave Steiner, but attacking Zhukov's flanks would have been suicide. Heinrici detached the 18th Panzer Grenadier Division – a division of *OKW* reserves – from Steiner on 16 April and assigned it to reinforce the Seelow Heights defenses. A few days later the 11th SS Volunteer Panzer Grenadier Division 'Nordland' was detached to cover Berlin, while the experienced 23rd SS Volunteer Panzer Grenadier Division 'Nederland' was detached to check Konev's advance. What Steiner had left were 20,000 men (naval crews from the Baltic ports, untrained high-school-aged children) and no artillery, tanks, fuel, or transport. Steiner refused to risk a confrontation with the Soviet armored column approaching Oranienburg under these conditions.

Late at night on 22 April, a three-hour meeting was held in the Chancellery bunker to clarify which engagements were in full swing to repulse the Soviet attack against the German capital. When Hitler asked where Steiner, who would break the siege, was, Krebs replied in all frankness: "Mein Führer, Steiner did not attack." Hitler was stunned for a while, and then threw a fit, insulting everyone and foaming with rage. Everyone present shuddered with fear.

Hitler once more berated the generals and his colleagues as "cowardly, dishonest, and treasonous," stressing the fact that he would remain in the Chancellery until the very end. He shouted, with his fists raised, crying: "It is all over. The war is lost. I will commit suicide." He then collapsed in a chair, still weeping.

# Waiting for Wenck

Hitler's staff realized that the Reich leader meant what he said: he truly intended to stay in Berlin and face the coming storm. He replied brusquely to his staff officers' pleas, who were begging him to change his mind and not abndon the Wehrmacht without a leader: "I have taken up a fixed decision. I cannot change it. I will defend Berlin to the end. I will either re-establish my command here in the capital or will fall with my troops." Two highest *OKW* staff officers and close colleagues of the Führer, Field Marshal Wilhelm Keitel and General Alfred Jodl, suggested a new plan that whetted his appetite. Hitler had ordered the re-forming of the 11th Army in the Harz Mountains in March, under Lieutenant General Walther Wenck. Its mission was to cover the huge gap created after the capitulation of the German armies in the Ruhr. The Americans had moved much faster than expected, however, and the counterattack Wenck meant to launch was cancelled because stronger forces pinned down the 11th Army. On 14 April Wenck succeeded in extricating his forces and, while falling back with the remnants of his Army, was ordered to form the 12th Army, incorporating some new 'ghost' paper-divisions. The Army arrayed the XLI, XXXIX, and XLVIII Panzer Corps and the XX Corps. In addition, many determined young troops, who had undergone a six-month training in officers' schools, as well as NCOs with significant battle experience, who had just convalesced from older wounds, were assigned to the new Army.

Wenck's new mission, as Hitler's trusted colleagues conceived it, was to meet with the cut-off 9th Army south of Berlin and to then hit the elite Soviet troops in their flanks, in order to isolate and eliminate them. At the same time, Lieutenant General Rudolf Holste's XLI Panzer Corps would move along the Elbe River to counterattack between Spandau and Oranienburg and Steiner would have to detach all his mechanized formations (7th Panzer and 25th

*Soviet T-34/85 medium tank of an unknown Red Army unit, Berlin, April 1945. The only marking on this tank is the slogan on the sides of the turret. This type was one of the most successful Soviet tanks during WW II. It was armed with an 85 mm main gun and two 7.62 mm machine guns as its secondary armament. A total of 44,000 T-34/85s were built and all the countries of the eastern coalition used them postwar. Finished in Russian Green. (Illustration by Dimitris Hadoulas / Historical Notes by Stelios Demiras)*

HADOULAS

*This young woman did not manage to save her life, although she sought refuge in one of the hundreds of tank turrets the Germans had placed around Berlin.*

Panzer Grenadier Divisions) to the new Army. Jodl would immediately leave Berlin for Berchtesgaden and Keitel for the 12th Army's headquarters in the forests of Wiesenburg, 100 kilometers southwest of Berlin. Goebbels and his family moved into the bunker the day the heads of the *OKW* left Berlin.

While Hitler was giving the impression of a pathetic psychopath, trying to hold on to his last chance, the Soviets were already at Köpenick, an eastern suburb of Berlin, and were approaching Spandau. They had also seized control of Berlin's Frankfurter Allee, occupying it as far as the Alexanderplatz. Weidling had spread his divisions from Pankow to the edges of the Tempelhof airfield, trying to cover all critical sectors, but his troops were extremely exhausted. The 9th Paratroop Division (Major General Bruno Bräuer), which was covering the northern sector, was but a remnant of its former self. The same was true of the Panzer Division 'Müncheberg' (Major General Werner Mummert).The 20th Panzer Grenadier Division, though faring a bit better than the other formations, had lost its commander, Major General Scholze, who had committed suicide when his formation reached Berlin. Only the 'Nordland' (SS Major General Zigler) and the 18th Panzer Grenadier Division (Lieutenant General Zutavern) remained battle

worthy and Weidling tried to block major approaches with them. He could also count on the firepower concentrated on three reinforced-concrete flak towers, located at the Berlin Zoo (Tiergarten), Humboldthain, and Friedrichshain.

The same day, Stalin made a decision on a more clear-cut definition of the inter-front boundary of the two Soviet fronts, assigning Konev the western sector of Berlin to the Anhalter Train Station, 150 meters from the Reichstag and Hitler's underground bunker. Zhukov, whose troops had already been engaged in street fighting in the eastern sector, was, then, going to finally be the 'Conqueror of Berlin,' as Stalin had promised five months before. It was the right moment, as, a few hours earlier, 8th Guards Army troops had reached the Spree River from the south and had managed to cross it with any means they could find, before the defenders even realized what had happened.

Nevertheless, the German resistance grew progressively tougher. "The SS attempted six attacks in three hours," a 3rd Shock Army divisional commander recounts, "but they were forced to retreat every single time, leaving the ground full of corpses in black uniforms." Hitler might have been entombed in his bunker, but he continuously demanded to be given details about the positions and movements of the two major formations that could still play a role in the Battle of Berlin (Wenck's 12th Army and Busse's 9th Army). In a rage, the dictator blamed these formations' inability to rush and help the capital (and himself), but both were fighting stubbornly in the western and southeastern suburbs of the city respectively, in a hopeless attempt to meet. On 24 April, after

Zossen was lost, Hitler placed all forces fighting in the Eastern Front under *OKW* command, believing that it was a better control scheme compared to *OKH*, which had had the Eastern Front operations under its command until then. Mere organizational re-arrangements could not salvage the situation for the Nazi state.

In his frenzy, Hitler made it easier for the Soviets. On the evening of 23 April, he ordered the LVI Panzer Corps, covering Busse's northern flanks, to retire to Berlin and to fortify itself in its eastern and southeastern approaches. This move brought the 8th Guards Army and the 3rd Guards Tank Army elements together on 24 April close to the Schönefeld airfield, at the southeastern edge of the city. The remnants of Busse's divisions, meanwhile, were encircled in a large triangular pocket (Beeskow-Senzig-Lübben) by five Soviet Armies (3rd Guards, 28th, 3rd, 69th, and 33rd) and couldn't rush to Hitler's aid. Keitel, who tried to visit the frontlines and see the situation for himself, realized that the *OKW* headquarters had moved to a farmhouse close to Fürstenberg while he was away.

As Konev approached Berlin from the south, his main problem was the Teltow Canal, a strong antitank obstruction, 50 meters wide and 3 meters deep. The Germans had blown up all the bridges over the canal and massed as strong a force as they could muster to retain this artificial barrier, covering 12 kilometers of frontline with 15,000 men, 250 guns and mortars, 130 armored vehicles, and more than 500 machine guns. Rybalko spent all of 23 April preparing to breach the Teltow Canal line, assembling 3,000 guns, rocket launchers, and mortars in a narrow three-kilometer front, to be used as an unprecedented 'hammer,' which

would obliterate the German defenses. The Soviets launched their attack at 0620 the next morning and by 1300, Soviet engineers had set up the first pontoons to ferry tanks across the canal. At the same time, the huge air fleets of the 2nd (Aviation General S. A. Krasovsky,) 16th (Aviation General S. I. Rudenko), and 18th Air Armies (Aviation General A. Ye. Golovanov) concentrated their sorties over the city, aiming mainly at keeping the Luftwaffe remnants away from the Berlin skies, to prevent ammunition and other supply drops to the beleaguered garrison.

Chuikov's troops crashed ran into the same enemy that checked their way from the Seelow Heights to Berlin: Panzer Division 'Müncheberg', a typical example of formations hastily formed during the last months with few troops and inadequate heavy weapons. "Russian artillery fires incessantly," an officer of that division writes. "The Russians open their way through buildings by using flame-throwers. The women's and children's shrieks are terrible. We only have 12 tanks and about 30 armored vehicles. We always get orders from the Chancellery to send tanks to another place in the city, but they never return." Three Armies of the 1st Belorussian Front penetrated into Berlin at the same time. In the area around Eberswalde, the German Army Detachment Steiner achieved a

*A Soviet soldier trying to take cover behind a burning T-34/85 that had fallen victim to the German anti-tank weapons. After the battle, Konev confessed that the Red Army had lost "more than 800 tanks" in the city.*

*Waffen SS troops march to seize a new position east of Berlin.*

local success, but it was not followed up, because the LVI Panzer Corps could not coordinate with the detachment.

The Soviets had not yet succeeded in completely encircling Berlin, whose western approaches remained open thanks to the stiff defense of Hitler Youth units at the bridges over the Havel River and in Spandau. The gap between Zhukov's and Konev's vanguards to the west of the German capital was 40 kilometers on 22 April, but it shrank to 25 kilometers on 23 April. The first rumors about Soviet patrols of the two Fronts meeting at various points were heard on 24 April. The great moment came on 25 April, however, when 4th Guards Tank Army elements met Zhukov's 47th Army units at Ketzin, on the Mitteland Canal. Zhukov had managed to encircle Potsdam in an iron ring, sealing the fate of the Third Reich capital , which was now cut off from the outside world.

News that a 5th Guards Army unit met an American unit at Torgau on the Elbe River reached Berlin the same day. There were more meetings soon and they were a chance for manifestations of Allied solidarity and celebrations between American and Soviet troops. The smooth approach of the Allied armies should have left no hope for the collapse of the anti-Nazi coalition that Hitler harbored, and marked the beginning of the end for bloodstained Berlin. Disintegration reigned in the Chancellery bunker. The place was cramped, but had large reserves of food and alcohol and "one could only see people drunk or sad," Colonel Ulrich de Maizière, who was present, recounts. "Men of all ranks were acting like they were insane. There was no more discipline."

# Fighting out of impetus

Hitler continued planning maneuvers on the bunker's map and dictating orders that could not be implemented to the 9th and 12th Armies, with an obstinacy and self confidence that both surprised and charmed people, ordering them to strike the enemy and move immediately towards Berlin. "Without effective command and control, the Wehrmacht fought instinctively, like a beheaded chicken," David Glantz writes. On 26 April, the Soviets fielded 464,000 men, 12,700 guns, 21,000 *Katyusha* rocket launchers and 1,500 tanks in the central Berlin perimeter, and they were all ready to crush the resistance on which Hitler's fanatical fighters, trapped in the city, insisted. The defenders were 45,000 soldiers, 40,000 *Volkssturm* and 3,000 Hitler Youth members. There was no news from units, except for the news that the main mass of the 9th Army had been encircled southeast of Berlin, until the elderly General Weidling, the 'missing' commander of the LVI Panzer Corps, showed up in a Berlin suburb and called from a phone box. He stormed into the Chancellery, a little later, protesting about the indictment of desertion with which he had been charged and Hitler, impressed with his fierce expression, appointed him Commander of the Berlin Defense Area (the third and last such appointment during those days).

Living conditions for the poor Berliners, caught in the crossfire, were nightmarish: thousands of people of all ages crammed into the huge concrete flak towers that dominated the city's central sectors, while others pushed and shoved to get into cellars or into the subway tunnels, where sanitary conditions were disgusting or non-existent. Food and water supplies were dangerously diminishing and the incessant hammering of the Soviet artillery destroyed the electricity and gas supply network, as well as the sewage system. The worst nightmare for non-combatants, however, was the unreliable second-line Soviet troops, which were in the front rear and were composed mostly of non-Russians or released prisoners of war, venting their rage on German civilians and treating innocent people of all ages and sex brutally.

### 11th SS PANZER GRENADIER DIVISION 'NORDLAND'

#### 1. OFFICER SS – UNTERSTURMFÜHRER (2nd LIEUTENANT)
On 1st May 1945 in Berlin, remnants of the 11th SS Panzer Grenadier Division ' Nordland' fought to the last man at the church near the Chancellery. He wears the standard-issue tunic, peaked cap in field gray, and M1944 'dot pattern' pants. Note the collar with the 'Sun Wheel' Rune divisional insignia and Norway sleeve patch. He sports an Eastern Front button-hole ribbon and a Tank Destruction Badge on his right sleeve. He is armed with the Walther Pistol P38, which, like the P08, was distributed to all ranks of the German Army. A remarkably robust weapon, it performed very well on the Russian Front in conditions of extreme cold that put other weapons out of action. It was accurate and easy to shoot well and was very popular for its effectiveness. (Illustration by Johnny Shumate / Historical Notes-Comments by Stelios Demiras)

#### 2. WAFFEN-SS SOLDIER
He wears a camouflage M1942 type smock 'plain tree' pattern and standard-issue trousers. Note the lace-up boots and canvas gaiters. His helmet is M1942 type and he is armed with the 7.92 mm *Karabiner Kar 98K* carbine. The Kar 98K was adopted as the standard bolt-action rifle for the new Wehrmacht in 1935. It was produced by the millions in a number of factories, and production continued until the end of the war in 1945. There were never enough automatic weapons to replace bolt-action rifles altogether. *(Illustration by Johnny Shumate / Historical Notes-Comments by Stelios Demiras)*

*The Soviets had a great advantage in the intensive use of their abundant artillery resources in the role of close support.*

## "We can still crush the enemy!"

Nine Soviet Armies surrounded the huge, impenetrable Berlin trap. Zhukov's and Konev's warriors fought in the suburbs of Reinickendorf to the north and Steglitz to the south, displaced the SS troops from the Schöneberg City Hall, seized Tempelhof and, using innumerable shells, burned the ground of Tiergarten park, where most German batteries were concentrated. Weidling's task of defending Berlin was impossible, since only five of the 22 divisions provided by the city defense plan were available. Moreover, he had no panzers and the last huge ammunition depot had been blown up. As David Irving writes: "The coming street battles would be fought between trained, professional Russian combat troops with the glint of final victory in their eyes, and a few thousand German flak soldiers, Volkssturm men, and police units."

Some good news reached Berlin during the same day, while the sudden pouring rain put out some of the fires that were raging. The good news was that the relief attack by Wenck's 70,000 men had finally begun and made some progress towards Potsdam, and that Schörner had just captured Bautzen and Weissenberg, causing heavy casualties to the 1st Belorussian Front. Hitler's staff sent a telegram to Admiral Dönitz on 26 April:

"Schörner's attack proves that, provided there is a will, we can still crush the enemy." In reality, Schörner had advanced but 24 kilometers during the first six days and another 10 during the next week, but would never be able to cover the other 54 kilometers to reach the surrounded 9th Army. The Führer's circle, having lost touch with reality, could not believe that the Soviets would succeed in seizing a metropolis such as Berlin, when they were losing 50 tanks a day. "The Russians have already exhausted their forces by crossing the Oder," Hitler said to himself, "especially the Northern Army Group (Zhukov's)." The enemy, however, did not seem to agree, as its troops came out of Tempelhof on 26 April and captured Belle Alliance Platz, the large boulevard reaching to the Brandenburg Gate, less than two kilometers from the Unter den Linden. Other Soviet attacks seized Zehlendorf and Dahlem in the south, Tegel and Wittenau in the north and also penetrated deep into the industrial suburb of Siemensstadt, where, up until a few hours earlier, German weapons were still being manufactured.

A giant smoke cloud enveloped the besieged city on 27 April and the only area still in control of the defenders was limited to a narrow strip of destroyed city blocks 16 kilometers long and 5 kilometers wide, from west to east. The Spandau area was already in Soviet hands, as was Neukölln in the south and the Gatow airfield, west of the Spree. A large Soviet assault had been progressing since 0500 along Hohenzollerndamm Strasse and the Anhalter station was later captured in the south. The advance continued to Leipziger Strasse and Prinz-Albert Strasse, where the Soviets seized the Gestapo headquarters. The

Chancellery was but 300 meters away, but the Germans viciously counterattacked, recapturing the Gestapo building, then losing it again to the Soviets, but they checked their advance for the moment. "Berlin is not a beautiful city," Colonel Pyotr Mitrofanovich Sebelev, an engineer with the Guards Tank Army in Siemensstadt, wrote to his family. "Narrow streets, barricades everywhere, broken trams and vehicles. The houses are empty because everybody is in the basements. The Germans have a starved and long-suffering look." Conditions were worsening for the fighters and the German soldiers quenched their thirst by drinking water from the canals, as there were but a few water pumps working.

Meanwhile, things were different for Chuikov's men, the Stalingrad veterans. While the Red Army was attacking with superior forces in aircraft, guns, and armor, the Germans set up masterful ambushes. Zhukov responded to the resistance with a rocket barrage. A huge explosion shook the city when a depot full of *panzerfaust* rocket launchers exploded in Potsdamer Platz, causing hundreds of casualties. This did nothing to deter the 8th Guards Army from crossing the Landwehr Canal on the afternoon of 27 April, nor pushing the Panzer Division 'Müncheberg' back to the Potsdamer Platz. This delay, however, gave the lead to the 3rd Shock Army fighters, who were coming down from the north.

French journalist and historian Raymond Cartier described the scene in Berlin: "A rain of ash is falling on Berlin. The cement and plaster dust raised by one million shells falls on the city mixed with smoke and the sparks of a sea of fires. One cannot see the sun... Flame arches cover the roads...

Shells are falling from all directions. The panting firing of Stalin's batteries throws earth and stones up in the air like large water jets. Huge quantities of rubble cover the roads that are full of potholes: cars, trucks, broken weapons, burned out tanks, even open suitcases with their contents spread around."

Life in such a hell was unbearable. "Except for programs on battery-operated radios and the few announcements for food distribution, most news went from mouth to mouth," Beevor mentions. "It was hard to distinguish facts from rumors. A nightmarish feeling, with no connection to reality, had stormed the city that was waiting for its sentence to be carried out, that bright and sunny spring day with its attendant pouring rain." The non-combatants' presence in this chaos rarely touched the attackers. "We had no time to see who is who," recounts a Soviet soldier. "Sometimes we were just throwing a hand grenade into an attic and then just went on." The atrocities against innocent civilians multiplied and rumors of gang rapes spread like fire, intensifying the feeling of terror. Soviet soldiers, wild from the battle heat, stormed into houses many times, confiscating food and valuables: their favorite loot were watches and liquor.

*The Chief of the Army General Staff (OKH), General Krebs, in a photo at the headquarters of the Soviet 8th Guards Army during the ceasefire talks. He committed suicide a few hours later.*

Hitler still tried to control the situation and demanded information on Wenck's movements. The attack launched on 27 of April surprised the Soviets with its strength and the accuracy of its blows. The 12th Army XX Corps seized Belzig, causing disorder in the Soviet rear and then the XLI Panzer Corps captured the important crossroad of Beelitz, where it released 3,000 German prisoners and wounded. It then tried to reach the town of Ferch, on the southern side of Schwielow Lake, 20 kilometers from Berlin. But it still could not penetrate the deadly ring tightening around the capital. The situation in the 9th Army sector was similar. The Army was trapped on the double bend of the Spree River, in a pocket with a perimeter of approximately 120 kilometers, and gave the impression that it was trying to move west and not northwest towards the city. Busse's strength was 200,000 men and, excepting 9th Army units, included a 4th Panzer Army corps that had been cut off north of Konev's penetration, and the Frankfurt an den Oder garrison that had succeeded in a heroic break from their besieged town.

Busse launched his attack on 26 April, after having moved the last 31 remaining panzers to the western side of the pocket, between Dahme and Zossen. This unexpected move took the Soviets by surprise and the Germans blocked the Baruth – Berlin highway. The 1st Belorussain Front troops (28th Army), however, responded fiercely and the battle raged violently for hours. The 9th Army managed to reach 37 kilometers from Beelitz, where Wenck's positions were, but it was exhausted by this superhuman effort and had critical shortages in weapons, fuel and ammunition. Its armored vanguard was cut off and eliminated close to

Luckenwald on 28 April, but it continued moving to the west, driven by despair-fueled courage. The Soviets tried to eliminate this rolling pocket, which was slowly moving west like a caterpillar between Beelitz and Luckenwald. In their attempt, they even tried to persuade the survivors to surrender by throwing 250,000 leaflets.

Two days later, when Berlin's drama was reaching its culmination, 30,000 of Busse's troops finally met the 12th Army and escaped being captured by the Soviets. The masterly escape moves of the 9th Army warranted comments of admiration. Even Konev, whose armies were in danger of being cut off at a certain moment of the operation, commented on it: "Comparing the operations of Wenck's 12th Army with those of the 9th Army, which was trying to break through to link up with it, I must say that the comparison is in favour of the 9th Army. After being severely mauled at an early stage, Wenck continued to fight, so to speak, according to protocol, just to carry out orders and no more, whereas the 9th Army, in trying to escape encirclement, fought bravely, to the death. And it was this determined fighting of theirs that gave us a good deal of trouble during the last days of the war."

Third Panzer Army remnants began withdrawing to the west on 26 April, leaving the area where the drama had unfolded, despite Heinrici's assurance that he would defend a line from Angermünde to Ockerheim. Keitel informed Hitler that Heinrici and Manteuffel were driving the 3rd Panzer Army (about 155,000 men) on purpose through Mecklenburg with the obvious intention of surrendering them to the Western Allies and not to engage them in the Battle of Berlin. With a wire, Wenck reported that he needed help

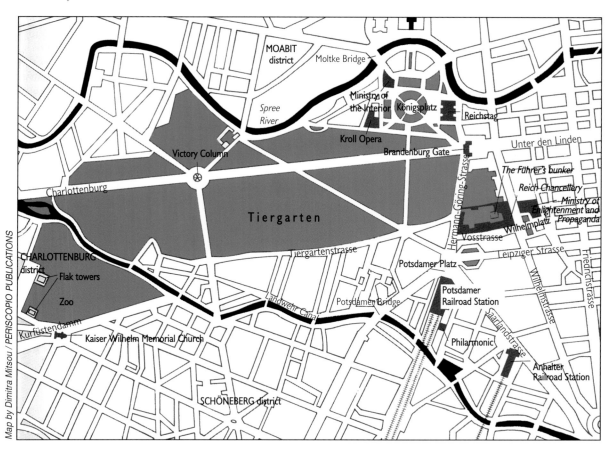

Map by Dimitra Mitsou / PERISCOPIO PUBLICATIONS

to move any further, but the only corps available (two divisions, under Reymann) had been pinned down north of Potsdam.

The city's defense had been assigned to motley disbanded units of the German Army, SS troops, foreign volunteers (the Danes, Norwegians, and Swedes of the 'Nordland'; the French of the 33rd SS Grenadier Division 'Charlemagne'; the Belgians of the 'Wallonien'; and others), as well as elderly or very young reserves of doubtful fighting value. Krebs spread the rumor that the Soviets had carried monster, 370 mm and 406 mm calibre, mortars close to the city, but, in the meantime, the defence lines had stabilized and Hitler Youth units still held onto a bridgehead south of the Pischelsdorf Bridge, waiting for the arrival of Wenck's forces.

The battles in Berlin moved to the Charlottenburg and Wilmersdorf sectors on 28 April, at a small distance from Tiergarten and Hitler's bunker. The fanatical defenders of National Socialism fought to hold the buildings that were once used by the German government, in the Wilhelmstrasse, Bendlerstrasse and around the Chancellery. "The famous Berlin Tiergarten (zoo) became a nightmare: birds were flying terrified and large animals were lying cut in pieces. The German civilians were trying to live like cave-dwellers, moving from cellar to cellar, while new fears were added to the terror they already felt, clinging to life and sharing some warmth and food, when the artillery firing stopped and Soviet infantry units stormed to clear a block, followed by a crowd of brutal and drunk rapists and looters...

*The center of Berlin (also called 'Fortress') in the greater area of Tiergarten was the heart of the defense, as Hitler was in the Chancellery cellars. The Soviets attacked from the Moltke Bridge in the south and slowly cleared the Reichstag and Chancellery areas, without realizing how close they were to the Third Reich leader.*

*The fall of the German eagle: two Soviet soldiers examining the inside of the seized Reichstag after the end of the battle.*

SS troops passionately hunted down deserters and hanged privates under orders from young hawk-like officers, who did not care for their pleas or excuses, even where the Soviet scourge had not arrived yet," historian John Erickson describes.

On the same day, the Germans fighting in central Berlin, between the Spree River and the Landwehr Canal, blew up the Moltke Bridge in an attempt to stem the northern Soviet advance, which was trying to reach the heart of this 'fortress,' as Hitler called it. The bridge was badly damaged from the explosion, but when the dust and the smoke subsided, it was discovered that its destruction was not complete. As a result, Kuznetsov's assault detachments from the 3rd Shock Army managed to cross it by midnight. Hard battles followed for the Königsplatz area, where some of the most important buildings of the city were concentrated, such as the Ministry of the Interior (Red Army troops called it 'Himmler's House'), the Kroll Opera and the Reichstag. "If there was no battle," a Soviet war correspondent writes, "the distance to the Reichstag was but a few minutes. Now it looked inaccessible, full of shell-holes, tram rails, pieces of wire and trenches."

Despite the Soviet soldiers' fear of getting killed during the last days of the war, they fought stubbornly to eliminate "the fascist beast in its lair," as their propaganda spread about. Private Vladimir Pereverzev wrote to his family: "Greetings from the front. I am alive and in full health until now, though drunk all the time. It is important to be courageous and to keep being so. We are tightening our noose around the center of the city now. I am only 500 meters from the Reichstag... You wrote that a part of the kitchen roof has collapsed, but that is not important! A six-story building fell on us here and we had to dig to get our comrades out. That is the way we live, giving blows to the Germans."

## The Führer's twilight

It is doubtful that Hitler had realized the end was coming. He seemed persuaded, until the night of 28 April that Wenck would manage to penetrate Berlin and repulse the Soviet attack. Indeed, he analyzed the tactics the 12th Army would follow and talked about the axes on which it would advance, without realizing that this Army had ceased to exist after it had been crushed by the Soviets. On the morning of 29 April, the battle could clearly be heard raging merely 800 meters from the frontline. The part of the building above ground level had been completely destroyed by Soviet artillery fire, but below, deep under the city, Hitler went on, making his last decisions.

He spent the first hours of the day dictating his 'political testament' to one of his secretaries, giving no answer, strangely enough, to the drama the German people and all of Europe was going through, but, rather, stressing the need for the fight against Bolshevism and the Jews to The incomprehensible attempt to justify his monstrous actions simply proved that he had not learned anything from what had happened and that he felt no obligation to give an account for the destruction he had caused. He then ordered three copies of his will to be made and sent by courier to the *OKW* headquarters, to Admiral Karl Dönitz and to Field Marshal Ferdinand Schörner. He also expressed his great respect for those two men and, after announcing his intention to commit suicide, he appointed the admiral as the new head of state and Schörner as Chief of the Armed Forces. On the other hand, he dismissed Speer, who had dared to disobey his explicit order to destroy Germany's infrastructure, and expelled Göring and Himmler from the Party – Göring because he rushed to consider himself the Führer's heir and Himmler because he began secret peace negotiations with the Western Allies. Finally, Hitler married his lover, Eva Braun, in a civil ceremony conducted by a city councilor, Walter Wagner, with Goebbels and Bormann as witnesses.

Hitler did not sleep during the night of 28 April and early next morning retired to his room, where he remained until the evening. Artillery fire, though, had reached the Führer's bunker and, as it hit the Chancellery, a deep and continuous thud filled the bunker's corridors. The Soviet advance continued making use of a variety of means and equipment. The strength of the buildings built with stone and concrete was an unpleasant surprise for the Soviets. As the battle raged, the Red Army began using heavy, 152 mm and 203 mm howitzers, shooting over open sights and bringing down walls for the riflemen to storm the buildings. Zhukov's troops reached the Bismarckstrasse, Kantstrasse, Saarlandstrasse, Wilhelmstrasse and, at the same time, crushed several isolated defense pockets at Pankow and Neukölln. The defense pocket had been squashed into a narrow piece of land from Alexanderplatz to Pischelsdorf Bridge and the Havel River but, despite being hammered for a long time, it showed endless reserves of strength. Soviet casualties

increased, and the defenders proved to be adept in the use of all kinds of anti-tank weapons. Alexanderplatz remained unconquerable, while the tanks that dared show up in Kurfürstendamm were all destroyed within a few minutes. Hitler Youth members, still in shorts, burned five T-34s down and then recaptured a building in Halensee, fighting for each room separately, without, however, taking any prisoners. Russian journalist Yelena Rzhevskaya, who toured the destroyed barricades and the rubble in a Jeep, wrote that "...the air became thicker as we were closing in on the center. Whoever was in Berlin that time, remembers that pungent, thick, ashy air, dark, full of smoke and dust from the rubble and the sand that ground between the teeth." High up, on the windows of

*The end of the Battle of Berlin and the collapse of National Socialist Germany caused an explosion of enthusiasm by Red Army troops in front of the famous Brandenburg Gate.*

the buildings, there were white bed sheets, put up as a sign of surrender.

Nevertheless, there were some fleeting moments of optimism and activity in the Chancellery bunker. At 1952 Hitler sent a message to Jodl by radio, asking him: "Where are Wenck's spearheads? When will they resume the attack? Where is the 9th Army? Where is it breaking through? Where are Holste's XXXXI Panzer Corps spearheads?" Then, at 2200, the trapped dictator held the night briefing conference, as he always did. It was but a formality, since the bunker had been completely cut off from the forces that were still fighting, as the balloon-suspended transmitting radio antenna had been destroyed in the morning, and the telephone exchange had ceased to function. What was left to be briefed on was the progress of the enemy's advance around the building and the Chancellery Commandant, SS Major General Wilhelm Möhnke, did that. At the same time, vicious battles were held at Anhalter Station, while the Soviet troops moved down the Saarlandstrasse and Wilhelmstrasse, dangerously approaching the Air Ministry. Weidling, who had managed to reach the bunker from his headquarters at Federstrasse with great difficulty, as heaps of rubble covered the roads, warned that ammunition supplies had began to run out and that the Soviets would, very probably, manage to break through the last defense line and reach the Chancellery by 30 April. "The Russians will be in position to spit on our windows in the morning." He asked to urgently allow the troops still fighting in the city to

*One of the bronze Chancellery plaques, riddled with bullets by the Soviet troops the day after the Red Army's triumphant victory in May 1945.*

attempt a break out to the west. Hitler rejected this request, as it was clear that he was more worried about his own end.

During the night of 29, April Hitler said farewell personally to each of his staff and his servants, beginning with the women (secretaries, nurses, and cooks), who had lived with him during these last desperate weeks and ending with the men (aides, party members, and officials). On the morning of 30 April and after getting a bit of sleep, he had lunch with his favorite secretaries, Gerda Christian and Traudl Junge, who had followed him in all his moves in the various underground headquarters, from Rastenburg and Vinitsa to Berlin. Then, with Eva Braun, he said farewell to Bormann, Goebbels, and the other high officials of his entourage, who had remained in the bunker. Hitler and his wife retired at 1530 in their private quarters, and bit on a cyanide capsule. Simultaneously, the dictator shot himself in the head with a 7.65 mm Walther PPK pistol.

# The red flag flies over the Reichstag

Stalin, unaware of the dramatic events taking place in the Chancellery, eagerly hoped for victory by May Day, in order to combine the triumph with the Party celebrations. But the German defenders did not give up easily. On the day Hitler committed suicide. The Soviet forces succeeded in dividing the German defenses into four pockets within the city and then began systematically eliminating them. It was a tough and tiring task, despite the clear superiority of the attackers, because the Soviets had to clear out the German fighters from 300 city blocks, where battles raged from house to house and floor to floor. One hour after Hitler had committed suicide, Zhukov's troops from the 1st Battalion, 756th Regiment, 150th Rifle Division, 3rd Shock Army climbed to the second floor balcony of the semi-destroyed Reichstag and placed one of the red flags with the hammer and sickle, distributed to the assault units by the political commissars.

Seizing the Reichstag would mark the end of the German defense of Berlin, but about 500 German soldiers were still fighting viciously in the building, although a mass of 89 heavy guns had been concentrated there and was firing at it. The building was extremely strong, despite having been built 50 years earlier. The battle continued unabated throughout the evening and the Soviet troops, using hand grenades and sub machine guns, separated the Germans into two separate parts by isolating some in the cellar and pushing others to the floors above. Late at night, at 2250, a final assault of the Soviets allowed two of their men, sergeants Mikhail Yegorov and Mel'ton Kantariya, to climb to the top of the Reichstag and unfurl their own flag next to the cupola. Both sides continued fighting, exhausted and thirsty, while dust and smoke choked them and took their breath away. The battle eventually ceased the next evening, when 300 dirty, unshaved Germans in tattered uniforms surrendered.

A tragedy of a larger scale took place a little later, when 'Nordland' sappers were ordered to blow up a wall between the Landwehr Canal and the subway tunnels, because Soviet troops were moving inside them. The Germans planned to flood the tunnels and check the Soviet advance. Thousands of civilians, who had sought shelter in the Anhalter Station tunnels were tragically trapped and tried to find a way out in the darkness,

*General Helmuth Weidling fought bravely to defend Berlin with the LVI Panzer Corps under his command, but he finally surrendered to the Soviets on 2 May 1945.*

to get away from the water that was rising up menacingly. Hundreds drowned, many children among them.

Hitler and Eva Braun were cremated according to their wishes in a shell hole in the Chancellery garden and were then buried in another shell hole from where the Soviets dug them up on 5 May. In the meantime, the battle still raged and Soviet shells often fell close to the Chancellery, forcing Goebbels, who was now acting Chancellor, to come into contact with the Red Army forces and ask for a truce, so that contacts for the capitulation could start. Late in the evening of 30 April, a lieutenant colonel was sent for that purpose to the closest Soviet headquarters and on the next morning Krebs, who spoke Russian, crossed the burning rubble in order to meet a highest Soviet officer and arrange the truce details. The officer Krebs met was no other than General Chuikov, the rock of defense in Stalingrad. Bizarre talks began between four sides about Berlin's fortune. After having been informed by Krebs about Hitler's suicide and his heirs' wish to capitulate, Chuikov passed on the news to Zhukov by telephone, who then called Stalin in Moscow. The Kremlin leader was abrupt: he categorically demanded on behalf of the USSR nothing less than unconditional surrender. He then retired to rest.

Zhukov, however, decided to look deeper into the matter and sent the 1st Belorussian Front Chief of Staff, General Vasily Sokolovsky, to Chuikov's headquarters to find out more. The two Soviet generals realized, after meeting again with Krebs, that an indescribable chaos reigned in the bunker and that Hitler's men had lost all contact with reality. On the evening of 1 May, Chuikov lost his temper with Krebs' formalities and made it clear that Goebbels and the new 'government' had no other choice but "the chance to make a public statement about Hitler's death and Himmler's treason and to declare Germany's absolute and unconditional surrender to the USSR, the USA and Great Britain." At the same time he sent the following message to his troops: "Fire as many shells as you can. No more talking. Clear the place up."

All Soviet guns and rocket launchers in the greater Berlin area opened fire at 1830 in the sector that still showed signs of resistance, sending a clear warning to those in the bunker. Two hours later, Goebbels and his wife committed suicide, after poisoning their six children. The rest of the Chancellery cellar residents were hastily organized in small escape groups and left the place. "The most cool-headed committed suicide," historian Cartier comments. "At the same time, the weaker ones tried to disappear into the mass of the civilians." Soviet troops, in the meantime, hesitated in risking the loss of more lives, naturally enough, when the war's end was so close. They slowly headed towards the Chancellery following the artillery barrage that continued demolishing the rubble and the people taking refuge around it. Indeed, some hundreds of German fighters continued resisting with unbelievable bravery: Charlottenburg had not yet been seized, battles still raged in Kurfürstendamm and the Panzer Division 'Müncheberg' viciously defended the Zoo in Budapesterstrasse, on the other side of the city. The LVI Panzer Corps sent a signal on the morning of 2 May asking for a ceasefire and at 0600 Weidling surrendered to the Soviets. The Soviets took him to Chuikov's headquarters at once, where he signed Berlin's capitulation and was then forced to send a signal to all German forces, ordering them to cease any resistance, accusing Hitler of "leaving in the lurch" those who fought to the end for him.

Weidling's surrender, however, was not the end of this tragic battle. Many German soldiers refused to surrender and gathered at Charlottenburg, where General Mummert, his wounded hand in a bandage, formed a column and began a heroic break out to the west, crossing the Spandau Bridge like a storm. The clashes of these indomitable fighters with the Soviet troops were terrible and bloody. Mummert was killed on 3 May and his troops mixed with the starving refugees. Some succeeded in reaching Döberitz and later linked up with the 12th Army.

# The price of victory

The Soviet guns finally fell silent on the evening of 2 May 1945. The silence that fell upon Berlin was haunting, more frightening than the din of the unrelenting battle that raged for days. "This cloudy, cold and wet day is the day of Germany's collapse," Grossmann wrote, "through the smoke, among burning ruins and the hundreds of corpses lying in the streets like garbage." The Red Army troops cheered, fired triumphantly in the air, ate lots of food and drank plenty of liquor and arrayed their tanks for inspection along the same roads that a few years before had reverberated to the parading men and machines of the Wehrmacht. The peace, however, which the Stalingrad fighters had won, had just risen from a city that reminded one of a vast cemetery. During the siege about 125,000 Berliners lost their lives – 11,000 from heart attacks and 6,400 from suicide as a way out of the misery, desolation and terror.

The German Army had ceased to exist after a horrible and uneven struggle. The Soviets claimed that they killed 458,080 Germans and that 479,298 had been captured. Seizing the 'corpse of Berlin,' characteristically called so by the historian Max Hastings, took its own toll on the Red Army, although it was a proud and historical victory. Between 16 April and 8 May 1945, Zhukov, Konev, and Rokossovsky's forces suffered a total of 352,475 casualties (78,291 dead and 274,184 wounded), almost one tenth of their total strength. In brief, the price of this battle, the crown of the impressive success of the Soviet arms during World War II, was the heaviest for the Red Army since Stalingrad.

Nevertheless, Berlin's fall did not, formally, mean the end of the war in Europe. The Germans still fielded the isolated Army Group North in Courland and significant forces were still fighting in East Prussia at the beginning of May 1945. In addition, there were more battle-worthy forces: the 12th Army west of Berlin, the 7th Army (five divisions) to the south of the Elbe River, at least 40 divisions in Austria and Italy, and the powerful 50 divisions of the Army Group Center (Field Marshal Schörner) in Czechoslovakia. The German troops had an extremely low morale, but were driven by their instinct of survival; they had to escape to the west and avoid being captured by the Soviets. Stalin launched three Red Army fronts against these forces, seeking to eliminate them, and Prague was seized on 8 May 1945. It was the last time that the Red Square in Moscow shook under the triumphant salute of 1,000 guns, as protocol dictated for every time a European capital was captured.

*The USSR flag is mounted on the Reichstag roof on 30 April 1945.*

# Hanna Reitsch

## The last flight to besieged Berlin

*1976. Legendary German Air Force General Adolf Gallant embraces 64-year-old Hanna Reitsch under a Junkers Ju 52 at an event organized for veteran aviators at the Düsseldorf airport.*

One of the last flights of a German aircraft to the besieged Third Reich capital was made on the morning of 27 April 1945. The aim of those on board was to come into contact with Adolf Hitler, who was trapped in the underground shelters of the Chancellery. The aircraft was forced to land on a street, between wreckage and shell holes, as the airfields of the city had been destroyed by Allied bombings or had already been seized by Soviet troops. Its pilot was a woman, Hanna Reitsch, an outstanding Luftwaffe test pilot and famous before World War II for her performance in the air.

Hanna Reitsch was born on 29 March 1912 at Hirschberg, Silesia. Her father was an ophthalmologist and she studied in the Kiel Medical School, but gave up her studies in 1933 and devoted herself to aviation. Her performance soon established her as a glider and aerobatic pilot and she mainly flew for films of the era. She set the women's world record for non-stop gliding (five and a half hours) in 1933 and that same year, extended it to 11.5 hours. In 1936 she set yet another record: the world record in non-stop distance flight for gliders, covering a distance of 305 kilometers. She also set the world's altitude record for women flying with a glider to a height of 2,800 meters and, three years later, she made the first crossing of the Alps in a glider.

Her feats very soon made her famous in Germany and she won the favor of the National Socialist Party higher officials, though she never got involved into politics. Reitsch was posted to the Luftwaffe Test Center at Rechlin in 1937 and became a chief test pilot, under Karl Franke, testing most German Air Force aircraft types. She specialized in tests on the Junkers Ju 87 Stuka, Dornier Do 17, as well as on the first German production helicopter, the Focke-Achgelis Fa 61. The petite, young pilot won the admiration of the crowd and the political leadership once more, demonstrating the helicopter in a

*Hanna Reitsch in an aircraft cockpit.*

series of flights inside a stadium during the 1938 Berlin International Motor Show.

Hanna Reitsch held Hitler in high esteem and he awarded her the honorary rank of Flying Captain (*Flugkapitän*) in 1937. With the outbreak of World War II, Reitsch flew more as a test pilot, flying all Luftwaffe military aircraft. On 27 March 1941 Reich Field Marshal Hermann Göring presented her the Luftwaffe Pilot Badge in Gold at a special ceremony in Berlin.

The next day she met Hitler in the Chancellery for the second time, after a special invitation. After the war, Reitsch wrote in her memoirs about this meeting: "The Führer greeted me warmly and amicably, while Göring was next to me, proud like a father presenting his daughter. Then, he asked me to sit next to him with the others round a large table. He asked me in detail about the test flights I flew, especially about my testing air brakes for diving. He also showed immense interest in my progress in experimental flights and the studies undertaken for cutting the cables of barrage balloons by aircraft and I was impressed, once more, by his knowledge of aviation and its development!"

*Fw 190A-8 serial 7+ ~ of the IV/JG54 displayed for the Berlin Air Defence in May 1945. This plane wears a camouflage typical of the last period of the war: Braunviolet 81/ Lichtgrün 83 over Hellgrau 76.*

Reitsch continued test flying intensively as the war raged, paying special attention to new aircraft designs and, mostly, to jets, like the Messerschmitt Me 163 Komet and the Me 262. She was awarded the Iron Cross 2nd Class in 1941 and the Iron Cross 1st Class in February 1944 by

Hitler in Berghof. She advanced a program for building manned V 1 flying bombs with a small cockpit in their fuselage. She test flew them, after the Normandy landings, in order for them to be used in suicide attacks against large Allied fleet units. The manned V 1s would be launched from He 111 bombers, which would carry them close to the target area.

# Flying to the besieged capital of the Third Reich

On 25 April 1945, just a few days before Berlin was seized by the Soviets, Reitsch was at Kitzbühel, where she received a message from Air Force

*Focke-Wulf Fw 190A-9 of the II (Sturm)/JG4, based at Mortitz during April 1945. The original painting overall RLM 76 with upper surface in RLM 74, RLM75 was partially on the fuselage, probably to adjust for combat damage. Note the new tail section and the radiator cowling of a different plane.*

General Ritter von Greim, commander of the 6th Air Fleet (*Luftflotte*), asking her to report to Munich in order to undertake a special mission. Hanna recounted later: "I climbed on a Ju 88 in Neubiberg and flew at 1400 on 26 April to the Rechlin air base. During the flight, I was informed that von Greim was ordered by a radio signal to report to Hitler in the Chancellery. The air force general decided that the only means possible to reach the Chancellery was the helicopter, since Berlin was under siege by Soviet troops. He also knew that only I would be able to fly such a daring mission, as I was familiar and experienced enough, having had already flown many times, day and night, over the city. I was one of the last people to have seen Adolf Hitler alive and one of the few to have survived and recount this event thanks to this flight, which was finally accomplished by other means..."

The situation in Reichlin was desperate. No German aircraft had managed to cross over the German lines and reach Berlin during the last two days. The only airfield close to the city that was still in German hands was Gatow, but it had been surrounded by the Soviets and was fired at incessantly by their artillery. Von Greim was waiting for Reitsch to arrive at the airfield so they could continue to Berlin together, but the helicopter they were going to use at night had just been destroyed in an enemy air raid.

*Il 2 Vindicator Ilyushin Il-2M3 Shturmovik of an unidentified unit seen in a famous picture taken during a strike mission over Berlin, on April 1945. The translation of the inscription on the fuselage is 'VINDICATOR,' a clear message for the Germans. It was a usual practice for the Russian crews to inscribe 'messages' on the fuselages of their aircraft. Standard scheme Dark Olive Green (FS. 34096) and Earth Brown (FS. 30118) over Light Blue Gray (FS. 35414).*

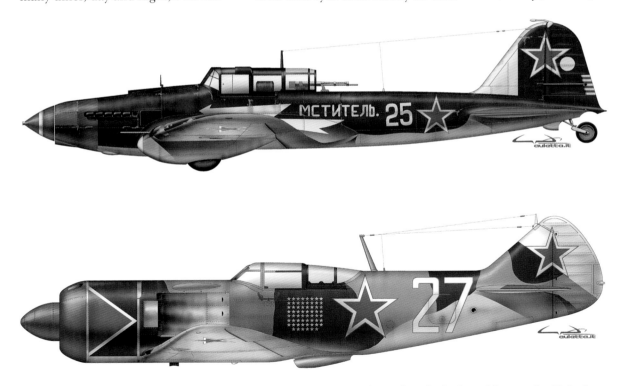

*Lavochkin La-7 of 176th GvIAP (Guards Fighter Aviation Regiment), 302nd IAD, flown by the Second Commander, Major Ivan Nikitovich Kozhedub on 17 April 1945 during a mission over the suburbs of Berlin. Flying with Lieutenant Dmitry Stepanovich Titorenko, hedecided to attack a group of 40 Fw 190s with bomb loads, flying to hit Russian troops. At the end of that mission Kozhedub reached the total of his personal Nazi downed planes of 62. The color scheme is Dark Gray (FS. 36187) / Medium Gray (FS. 36270) over Light Blue Gray (FS. 35414). This was the standard scheme for fighters after 1943, later the Light Blue Gray (FS. 35414) was changed with Light Gray (FS. 36622).*

*Hanna Reitsch on the cockpit of a glider, ready for a trial take off from a ship's deck.*

The only aircraft in Rechlin available for that flight was a specially modified Focke Wulf Fw 190 fighter, which had had a second seat added behind and below the cockpit. Its pilot was a Luftwaffe flying sergeant, who knew the defensive tactics and the positions of the Soviet anti-aircraft guns around the German capital very well, and who, two days earlier, had flown the Minister of Armaments, Albert Speer, to Berlin from the areas of Germany not occupied by the enemy.

Reitsch insisted on joining Von Greim and the sergeant to Berlin and the young sergeant, who admired her greatly, decided that the small woman's weight would not be a burden for his flight. Von Greim, unaware that Reitsch was about to join the flight, sat in the second seat and the only place left for Reitsch was a small compartment in the tail of the aircraft between hydraulic accumulators, rudder cables and oxygen bottles. Hanna did not dare reveal her presence until the airplane took off and soon found herself in the dark, not able to move, nor come out without help.

The flight to Gatow was short, luckily enough, and the Fw 190 took off with the escort of several Luftwaffe fighter planes. The plane then flew into the night to the distant horizon lit by the unceasing artillery barrage. Their destination was not only the besieged capital of the Reich, but history itself.

The first part of the 30-minute flight was fairly smooth and the aircraft reached the suburbs of Berlin flying at medium height. It landed in a small emergency landing field after having avoided a Soviet fighter

*28 May 1941. Adolph Hitler receives* Flugkapitän *Reitsch in the Chancellery after she was awarded the Gold Luftwaffe Pilot Badge.*

squadron which tried to attack it at the last moment. Von Greim and Hanna would continue with a small three-seater Fieseler Fi 156 Storch, hoping to be able to land on a road close to the Chancellery.

The air force general insisted on flying the airplane himself, because they would probably meet strong enemy defenses during their flight and Reitsch had no combat flight experience. Hanna sat in the back seat and, instinctively, tried to reach the control wheel, realizing that she could do it, though with great difficulty. The Storch finally took off a little after 0600 on 27 April, having some trouble from the enemy artillery. The little airplane flew low to avoid Soviet fighters over the Wansee Lake and then brushed by the trees of Grunewald Forest.

All of a sudden, as they were flying over a large clearing in the forest, the ground came alive and a volley of fire was thrown at them. Soviet tanks, armored vehicles and hundreds of troops fired at the sky with guns, machine guns, rifles and submachine guns trying to hit the Storch. The aircraft rolled and tossed, surrounded by tracer shells, bullets and smoke clouds from low-range shell explosions. Reitsch could clearly hear the sound made by shrapnel and shells crossing the fabric cover and the metallic parts of the plane. A little later, the air force general shuddered when a round from a heavy gun crushed the bones of his right leg.

Von Greim lost consciousness and Hanna came forward over the back of his seat, grabbed the Storch's controls and managed to keep it in the air. She could see the fuel leaking through the punctured fuel tanks in the wings and waited in agony for the explosion that would tear the plane apart. However, the Storch kept flying, miraculously

enough, passed close to a flak tower, then found itself in the eastern part of Berlin, close to the Brandenburg Gate and managed to land on a street in the German-held part of the city.

The area seemed deserted and Reitsch remained in the aircraft, trembling over the unconscious air force general, until an Army truck showed up to pick them up. After a short ride in the center of the city, through the rubble and the roads riddled with shell-holes, they reached the building of the Chancellery, the greatest part of this impressive construction lying in a dark mass of ruins, full of smoke and dust. Some SS guards escorted the two aviators into the cellars beneath the building, where Hitler's personal doctor, Dr. Ludwig

*A daring, but also deadly, challenge for test pilots of all times. Reitsch in the small cockpit of a manned V 1 bomb.*

*Flying Germany's first helicopter, the Focke-Achgelis Fa 61, inside a Berlin stadium, during the 1938 Berlin International Motor Show.*

*A visit to the Italian-occupied Libya before the beginning of the war. The petite and famous aviatrix oversees the preparations of her glider for a local flight.*

# With Hitler in the Chancellery cellars

Frau Goebbels met the newly arrived visitors, hugged Hanna in tears, although they had never met before, and all together they entered Hitler's private quarters. Reitsch and von Greim were shocked when they met him. Hanna recounts: "His head sagged to one side, his hands were constantly trembling. His eyes were beady and looking to the non-existent horizon, but they shone when he welcomed us. After the air force general's report, Hitler grabbed my hands and said full of enthusiasm: Brave woman! So, there still are faithful and determined people in our world."

Then, without wasting time, he addressed von Greim: "I called you here to tell you that I renounced

Stumpfegger, dressed von Greim's wounds. Then, Hanna and the wounded general, who was put on a stretcher, were led two levels below, to Adolf Hitler's personal underground quarters.

*Lavochkin La-7 of the 9th GFAR, flown by Maj. A. V. Alelyukhin as it appears during the Berlin Operation in the spring 1945. This La-7 was donated (note the donor's inscription on the fuselage) and it wears a non-standard camouflage with upper surfaces overall Medium Gray (FS. 36270) over Light Blue Gray (FS. 35414). Note also the personal emblem on the cowling.*

*Messerschmitt Me 262A-1a/Jabo serial 3 of the III/JG7 based at Briest, Berlin Area during spring 1945. The pilot was the Hptm. Erich Mikat, Gerschwaderadjutant of the JG7. Standard Braunviolet 81 (FS. 34088) and Lichtgrün 83 (FS. 34138) over Hellgrau 76 (FS. 35622).*

Hermann Göring because he has betrayed both me and his Fatherland... I should never have trusted him. I expect from you to restore the Luftwaffe's honor, which has been tarnished by Göring, who does not deserve to command it. Now, von Greim, I name you Commander-in-Chief of the Luftwaffe with the rank of Field Marshal."

Von Greim stood up, dumbfounded, not only for his sudden promotion but, mainly, for the way it was announced to him. He had abandoned his duties to report to Berlin, in constant danger of getting killed or captured by the Soviets, while a radio message by Hitler ordering him would have been enough. The Führer, most probably, wanted to

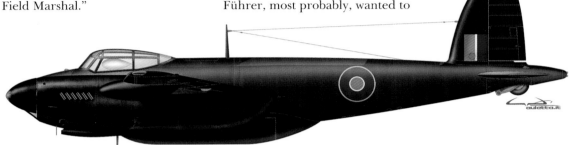

*De Havilland DH.98 Mosquito Mk XVI of the No. 608 Squadron, RAF. To reduce the visibility of the aircraft to the German AA artillery, the 608's Mosquitos were over painted in black on the lower surfaces and on the tail. Also the ID codes were covered. During all the Battle of Berlin little sections of Mosquitos were active, during the night, over the Berlin Area. They operated almost as Pathfinders for the units of Halifaxes and Lancasters.*

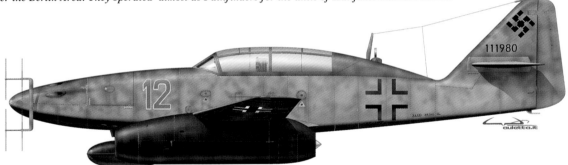

*Messerschmitt Me 262B-1a/U1 serial 12 (Werk Number 111980) of the 10./NJG 11 'Kommando Welter' flown in the spring 1945 by Lt. Herbert Altner. Based at Reinfeld, the NJG was one of the night-fighter unit deployed for the defence of the Berlin Area against night bombing missions. The camouflage of this well documented plane was overall* Hellgrau 76 **(FS. 35622)** *oversprayed in* Mittelgrau 75 **(FS. 36132)** *with undersurfaces in* Schwarz 22 **(black)**. *The upper surfaces of the wings were painted in* Lichtgrün 83 **(FS. 34138)**.

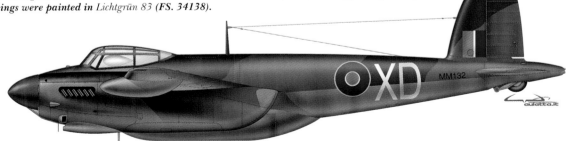

*De Havilland DH.98 Mosquito Mk XVI, serial XD (MM132) of the No. 139 'Jamaica' Squadron Pathfinders, RAF and flown by S/L (Pilot) Robert Joseph George Green (DFC & Bar) and F/L (Nav.) John Henry Robson (DFC). On returning from Berlin for a bombing mission, in extremely poor visibility, the Mosquito crashed about one mile short while making a beam-guided approach to Little Staughton. Operation Berlin, 15 January 1945.*

*Fieseler Fi 156 Storch aircraft, similar to the one Reitsch landed on a Berlin road on the morning of 27 April 1945.*

*Air Force General Ritter von Greim flew with Hanna Reitsch in the last flight from besieged Berlin, after their three-day stay in the Chancellery bunker, in the end of April 1945.*

stress the fact of an officer's promotion to the highest rank, given the fact that he had vowed to never promote anyone, after Paulus' surrender in Stalingrad.

Reitsch and von Greim remained in the Chancellery cellars for the next three days as the battles between the defenders of Berlin and the Soviet troops raged in the area around it.

During that time there were persistent rumors about Göring's conspiracy against Hitler. Hanna spent some of her time playing with the children of the Goebbels family, who were staying with them in several quarters of the underground shelter. She tried in vain to persuade their parents to allow her to carry them out of Berlin to a safe place. After Hitler's death, in fact, Frau Goebbels poisoned her children and she and her husband committed suicide.

Reitsch, like most Germans, was unaware of Hitler's private life,

believing that his unique occupation was governing the country and conducting the military operations. That is why she was rather surprised when she met his lover of 13 years, Eva Braun, who often told her: "I'm happy to die here... with the Führer! Now I have everything."

Everyone waited for the end sorrowfully in this last Berlin fortress. Indeed, Hitler distributed vials of poison, preparing his select partners and friends for a mass suicide, in spite of Hanna and von Greim's discrete proposals to help him escape by air to areas of Germany not yet occupied by the enemy. The chance Reitsch was waiting for in order to get out of the besieged Chancellery soon came, when rumors spread that Himmler had begun secret negotiations with the Allies about capitulation. A little after midnight on 29 April, Hitler, wild with rage, showed up in the entrance to Hanna and the wounded air force general's quarters and told them : "Himmler betrayed me! You two must leave the soonest possible from here... My information is that the Russians are going to break into the Reich

Chancellery tomorrow morning." He then assigned Himmler's punishment to von Greim.

The dynamic nature of Hitler's order, however, was not mirrored in von Greim's state of mind. He found it very difficult to move due to his severe wound and could only walk a few steps with the help of crutches, suffering in pain. They were soon informed that a light Arado Ar 96 liaison aircraft was heading for Berlin and so bid Hitler and everyone that was in the bunker farewell. Eva Braun and Magda Goebbels asked Reitsch to carry some letters. Escorted by General Hans Baur, they went up to the surface where the practically demolished building once stood. An armored vehicle drove them to the Victory Column where an Ar 96 was waiting for them. The pilot was the same sergeant who had flown them to the Gatow airfield with the Fw 190 three days before.

Despite the tens of anti-aircraft searchlights lighting up Berlin's dark sky and the fire of the Soviet artillery, the little airplane managed to take off without being spotted and, flying low, headed for Rechlin, where it landed a little after 0300. It was the last flight out of besieged Berlin. The next day, Hitler's death and the assumption of power in the Third Reich by Admiral Dönitz were announced on the radio.

# Epilogue

Hanna was back at Kitzbühel eight days Later, when Germany's unconditional surrender was announced, and with it the end of World War II in Europe. She was arrested by American troops and, although not in the military, she was accused by the Allies of being a war criminal and was kept in confinement for 15 months. Rumors that she had

smuggled Adolf Hitler out of Berlin by airplane led, during her detention, to her being heavily interrogated by the Americans about her presence in the Chancellery underground cellars in the end of April 1945 and her relationship with the National Socialist leadership.

Hanna started flying gliders again during the 1950s in West Germany. She achieved more distinctions and records, some still standing today. She flew a glider a distance of 802 kilometers, setting a world's record (Women's Out and Return World Record) in 1979, shortly before her death of a heart attack on 24 August that year at the age of 67.

*Hanna Reitsch after having been awarded the Iron Cross 1st Class in 1944.*

# The last days of the war in the *Führerbunker*

The Soviet Highest Command was not aware that Hitler and many highest officials of the regime were in the Chancellery underground shelter when the Battle of Berlin began. However, the Soviet attacks converged to the government ministries district. Enemy troops had to face determined defense by foreign volunteers from many different countries of Europe, as they were approaching the Chancellery, the Reichstag, and the Third Reich ministries.

The office of the German Chancellor was in the old Radziwill Palace in Wilhelmstrasse in the center of Berlin. The German Chancellor bought this building, built in the beginning of the 18th century, after the Unification of Germany. An extension of the building was constructed during 1929-30 and Hitler added a balcony to it in 1933. Three years later, an air raid shelter was built in the garden of the building. The new Reich Chancellery was built in 1938 along Vossstrasse, extending

*The Reichstag building after the end of hostilities.*

from Wilhelmstrasse to Hermann-Göring-Strasse (the latter street was parallel to Wilhelmstrasse and connected the Vosstrasse with the Brandenburg Gate).The new Chancellery underground cellars could be used as an air raid shelter. A tunnel was built, after the beginning of the war, to connect the first air raid shelter with the new Chancellery.

The Hochtief Company was called in to reinforce the initial air raid shelter in 1943, as Berlin had become a target of consecutive, powerful air raids. The same company built a new air raid shelter in 1944. It was built deeper than the first one, at a depth of

17 meters, with a 2.8-meter-thick ceiling and 2.2-meter-thick walls, much thicker than the initial shelter. It became quarters for Hitler and his entourage during the last days of the Third Reich, though it was never completed as planned.

The new shelter (*Führerbunker*) was connected with the old one (*Vorbunker*) with a staircase. A wall and a steel door, always guarded by two men, divided the two shelters. The *Vorbunker* was still used after the *Führerbunker* was built. Four of its rooms were given to the Goebbels family with its numerous members, while two rooms were given to the

**SOVIET RIFLEMAN, MOTOR RIFLE REGIMENT 1945**
*The telogreika (quilted winter jacket) was highly efficient for field wear in winter combat, particularly for troops being transported on tanks. Motor Rifles of the Red Army were frequently short of motor transportation and rode T-34 or other Russian tanks into action as tankoviy desant and dismounted to fight on foot when necessary. The M1940 shapka-ushanka cap in fleece-trimmed cloth was popular and efficient in the coldest climates. It was even seen worn under the steel helmet and was copied by the German Army and later by many other armies. A gasmask bag is sling over the right shoulder. He fires a PPSh-41 7.62 mm submachine gun with 71-round magazine. (Illustration by Johnny Shumate / Historical Notes - Comments by Stelios Demiras)*

BUNKER EXIT

*A 1945 air photo. The Führerbunker emergency exit to the Chancellery garden is clearly visible. In the foreground is Wilhelmstrasse and vertical to it is Vosstrasse. To the right (in the middle) is the Old Chancellery and on the top the edges of Tiergarten can be made out.*

service personnel. Other rooms were for food supplies and refrigerators, a wine cellar, a small generator, kitchens and the kitchen for Frau Constanze Manziarly, who cooked the Führer's special diet.

The *Führerbunker* consisted of 20 small rooms. There was a small corridor behind the door, separating it from the *Vorbunker* and its first section was a lounge/waiting room. This room was covered from wall to wall with a red carpet, its walls were decorated with paintings and there were elegant chairs lining them. The two doors to the right led to the generator/ventilation plant and to the telephone switchboard, while the first door to the left led to the washrooms. The second section of this corridor was a conference room and was connected to the first with a door. Hitler's personal doctor, Dr. Ludwig Stumpfegger, had his surgery on the right (including a small operating room and a bedroom), but Dr. Goebbels used it after the doctor's departure. On the left of the corridor were Hitler's office, a small conference room and two cloak-rooms. Hitler's private quarters were an office, a bedroom and a bathroom and they were connected with Eva Braun's apartment. These six rooms were painted light gray and the furniture was simple and practical. Hitler's office was small (3 meters x 4 meters) and depressing. There was an Anton Graff painting of Frederick the Great on the wall. The corridor led to an anteroom and then to the emergency exit, which, in turn, led to the Chancellery garden in the northwestern edge of the *Führerbunker*. The SS *Begleitkommando des Führers troops*, under SS Major General Johann Rattenhuber, were Hitler's personal Guard, the *Reichssicherheitsdienst (RSD)*. (See note 1)

A staircase and a 36-meter corridor led from the kitchen/dining hall of the old Chancellery to the *Vorbunker*, which was connected with tunnels with the new Chancellery building (to the south) and the buildings of the Ministry for Public Enlightenment and Propaganda (east, on the other side of the Wilhelmstrasse) and the Foreign

Ministry (north). The bunker was an independent complex with its own electricity and water supply, provided by an artesian well. A diesel-powered generator was used to power the ventilation plant in order to clean the air in such an enclosed place. The Siemens Company had installed a small phone exchange (of a size suitable for a medium size hotel or a divisional headquarters) in a room with enough space for a single telephone operator and a medium range Army radio was placed in the adjoining room. The Army *Zentrale 200* communications station in the capital zoo connected the bunker with the *Zentrale 500* in Zossen, 19 kilometers south of Berlin.

Hitler left the Chancellery and moved into the bunker with his faithful valet, SS Major Heinz Linge, during the first days of April 1945. On 20 April, the highest Third Reich officials gathered in the bunker for Hitler's birthday, but their visit was short. Ministers Hermann Göring, Heinrich Himmler, Albert Speer, and Joachim von Ribbentrop, *OKW* heads Wilhelm Keitel and Alfred Jodl and Rear Admiral Karl-Jesco von Puttkamer (the naval adjutant to Hitler) left during the next three days. Hitler's adjutant, Lieutenant General Julius Schaub, and his personal doctor, Theodor Morell, followed them. Life in the *Führerbunker* became dull at the end of April and all activity depended on Hitler's erratic program. The aides carried numerous documents and the secretaries had to type them on special typewriters with large letters, so that Hitler could read them without wearing glasses. The indifferent guards, who were not allowed to smoke or talk loudly, silently worried about their loved ones, contemplating the desperate situation.

*The Chancellery western entrance. The eagle was designed by Professor Kurt Schmid Ehmen. Leibstandarte SS 'Adolf Hitler' troops were its permanent guard.*

Zossen was seized by the Soviets on 22 April and the modern communications center ceased functioning. A balloon-suspended radio antenna was lifted over the bunker and communications were restored for the time being. Zhukov and Konev's armies met southeast of Berlin on 24 April, forming a suffocating ring around the city and the Chancellery area came into Soviet artillery range on 26 April.

## The *Führerbunker's* first casualty

The *Führerbunker* sustained its first 'casualty' on 26 April. SS Lieutenant General Hermann Fegelein, a former

*Probably, the only photo of the inside of the bunker. Vice Admiral Karl-Jesko von Puttkamer with members of the guard.*

jockey and a Waffen-SS cavalry commander, brother-in-law to Eva Braun and representative of the SS chief Heinrich Himmler to Hitler's headquarters, decided to abandon his Führer. Taking advantage of a quiet moment, he slipped away from the bunker without being seen. His absence was not noticed, but the next day Hitler asked for him, for no apparent reason. An SS detail was organized at once to find him and bring him back to the bunker. They did not have to search much, as

Fegelein was in his apartment, close to Kurfürstendamm, dressed in civilian clothes. He was led before Hitler, accused of desertion, was cashiered and, finally, confined to his room, in one of the Chancellery cellars.

Heinz Lorenz, Hitler's Chief Press Secretary, delivered a copy of a press communiqué by the Reuters international press agency on 28 April. It referred to the contact Himmler had had a few days earlier with the Swedish Count Folke Bernadotte in his attempt to negotiate Germany's capitulation. Hitler, who used to call Himmler "der treue Heinrich" (the faithful Heinrich) and thought that he could always count on his absolute devotion to him, was outraged and thought there was a connection between Fegelein's desertion and the SS leader's plot. SS Lieutenant General Heinrich Müller, the Gestapo chief, interrogated Fegelein, who confessed that he knew about the secret talks between his chief and the

*Bunker diagram*

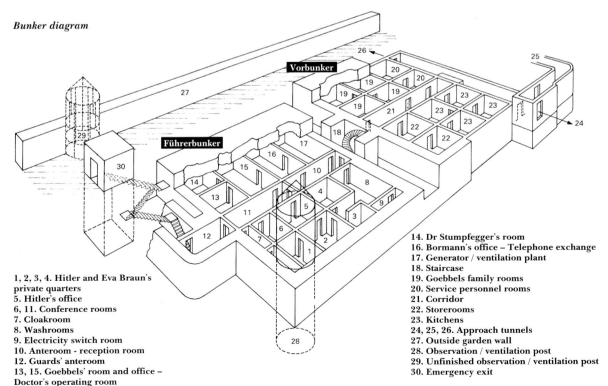

1, 2, 3, 4. Hitler and Eva Braun's private quarters
5. Hitler's office
6, 11. Conference rooms
7. Cloakroom
8. Washrooms
9. Electricity switch room
10. Anteroom - reception room
12. Guards' anteroom
13, 15. Goebbels' room and office – Doctor's operating room

14. Dr Stumpfegger's room
16. Bormann's office – Telephone exchange
17. Generator / ventilation plant
18. Staircase
19. Goebbels family rooms
20. Service personnel rooms
21. Corridor
22. Storerooms
23. Kitchens
24, 25, 26. Approach tunnels
27. Outside garden wall
28. Observation / ventilation post
29. Unfinished observation / ventilation post
30. Emergency exit

*SS-ROTTENFÜHRER (**CORPORAL**),*
*33rd WAFFEN GRENADIER DIVISION*
*OF THE SS 'CHARLEMAGNE' (1st*
*FRENCH), BERLIN, APRIL 1945*
*The grenadier's uniform is the standard*
*issue of the German Army after 1943. The*
*SS rank badge is on the collar and on the*
*left arm behind the eagle is a patch with*
*the colors of the French flag. Lower are the*
*corporal's chevron and the Charlemagne*
*cuffband. His steel helmet in dark gray is*
*M1942 type and the canvas magazine*
*pouches are the M1944 type for the*
*7.92 mm Sturmgewehr 44 (StG 44)*
*assault rifle with 30-round*
*magazine. The StG 44 was a*
*revolutionary weapon, the*
*ancestor of all of today's assault*
*rifles (small-caliber weapons with*
*full-automatic capability that fire a*
*short, powerful round). He is holding an*
*anti-tank weapon, a Panzerfaust 60.*
*The Panzerfaust was a single-shot 'throw-*
*away' anti-tank rocket launcher. Its*
*explosive head could penetrate any tank of*
*the period at short range. (Illustration by*
*Johnny Shumate / Historical Notes-*
*Comments by Stelios Demiras)*

*One of the last Chancellery defenders lies dead on the staircase of its western entrance.*

Swedish count. Fegelein was led to the Chancellery garden where he was executed, after short and formal procedures. After that, Hitler issued orders for Himmler's arrest and then he dealt with his personal affairs for the rest of the night: his marriage to Eva Braun and dictating his last will and testament.

The wedding ceremony was held in the early morning of 29 April, in the little conference room of the *Führerbunker*, by Inspector Walter Wagner, who presented himself in the uniform of the Nazi Party with a *Volkssturm* armband (he was killed when he tried to return to his unit). After signing the necessary register, the Hitler couple was congratulated by those present and, then, retired to their private quarters where they drank champagne with Martin Bormann, the Goebbels couple and two of his secretaries, Gerda Christian and Traudl Junge. Hitler and Junge retired to another room and he dictated his personal and political testament, while the celebration was going on. The communications balloon, through which all messages between the bunker and the outside world were sent, was shot down on the morning of the same day. After this break of communications, the aides had no reason to be present at the bunker. Major Bernd von Freytag - Löringhoven, Captain Gerhardt Boldt and Lieutenant Colonel Rudolf Weiss asked for permission to leave the

bunker. Each of the three men undertook the mission of carrying a copy of Hitler's political will through the Soviet lines to the new head of the Army, Field Marshal Ferdinand Schörner and to the Grand Admiral Karl Dönitz, who was appointed as Supreme Commander of the Armed Forces. Goebbels (the new Chancellor) added an appendix of his own to one of the copies, hoping that it would reach Munich, the cradle of National Socialism, and that he would earn mentions in history for it. Hitler ordered the three couriers to try their best to reach General Walter Wenck's lines, since they had no news from him. They were to tell him to rush to the Chancellery, because the defense was soon going to collapse. The three men left the shelter in the evening.

The battle was raging on ground level and the ring was tightening around the government buildings area. Its defense was going to be taken over by the French, Danes, Norwegians, and the Swedes. A telegram was sent on the night of 23 to 24 April 1945 from the Chancellery to SS Major General Dr. Gustav Krukenberg, Commanding Officer 33 SS Grenadier Division 'Charlemagne' (see note 2): 'Charlemagne' Division to utilize all possible transport for immediate movement to Berlin, AH."

About 1,100 French volunteers (from an initial strength of about 7,500 men) had been gathered in Carpin, in the wooded area of Mecklenburg, to rest and refit after the fierce battles in the Eastern Front. Krukenberg had released those who did not want to continue fighting from their vows of allegiance (see note 3). He needed but an hour to form an assault battalion (*Sturmbataillon*). It was composed of the available elements of the 57th Grenadier Battalion and the 6th Company / 58th Battalion under

*30 April 1945: Soviet troops attack the Reichstag.*

Captain Rostaing. Veterans of the Divisional Battle School *(Kampfschule)* under the German SS First Lieutenant Wilhelm Weber were added to this unit. The French jumped onto two light trucks and nine heavily laden trucks. Two of these did not reach their destination, due to difficulties along the way.

About 300 to 350 French officers, NCOs and grenadiers reached the northwestern suburbs of Berlin on 24 April, a few hours before the German capital was completely encircled. They headed for the Reichssportsfeld, in Charlottenburg, where they regrouped and replenished with a cache of supplies abandoned by the Luftwaffe. In the meantime, Krukenberg went on by car to the Chancellery for further orders. On the next day, the unit was reorganized into a reduced headquarters, under the SS Captain Henri Joseph Fenet, with four rifle companies, numbered 1 to 4, each comprising of 60 to 70 men. The unit moved east among the city rubble and under constant Soviet bombardment to the southern suburb of Neukölln. Fenet and his troops

were tactically attached to the 'Nordland' Division, of which Krukenberg had taken command.

The 11th SS Volunteer Panzer Grenadier Division 'Nordland' had received its last order on 16 April: to take defensive positions east of Berlin. The division was forced to fall back on 22 April, fighting to the center of the city and many of its subordinate units were isolated from their parent division and had to fight as independent units out of the city limits. 'Norge' and 'Danmark' Regiments (see note 4), as well as 11th SS Engineer Battalion *(SS-Pionier Battalion)* sub-units were posted at the Spree River bridges, the northern natural border of the capital center. The last operations for the seizure of the Spree canals began on 25 April. The grenadiers and the engineers, however, realized that it was impossible to check the numerous Soviet assault groups that were crossing the river with inflatable boats. Most of the survivors were forced to fall back south to the government buildings area on 26 April. The 'Nordland' Division ceased to exist as

*The round swastika (Sonnenrad) and the tactical marking indicate this leichte Schützenpanzerwagen (SdKfz 250/1) belongs to the reconnaissance unit of the Division 'Nordland,' while the number on the open back door that it was a 3rd Company vehicle, the one with the Swedish volunteers. It is rumored that this particular vehicle was used for the last escape attempt from Berlin, with company commander Captain Pehrsson as its leader. He was captured, but managed to escape from the Soviet Union two years later. The unlucky driver, Ragnar Johansson, lies dead on the road (right), probably on Friedrichstrasse.*

an organized formation in the capital. Its Commanding Officer, SS Major General Joachim Ziegler, was deemed incompetent in dealing with the desperate situation, and Dr. Krukenberg replaced him after an immediate order to that effect by the Berlin Commandant, Artillery General Helmuth Weidling.

The French volunteers engaged the enemy as soon as they reached Berlin. The largest part of the French unit took part in the first counterattack at Neukölln (Sector 'C' of the city's defence plan) on the morning of 26 April, supported by the heavy tanks and the self-propelled guns of the SS Panzer Regiment 'Hermann von Salza' (see note 5). Fenet was wounded in the leg during that battle. Brief and violent counterattacks at Hasenheide and the Tempelhof airfield followed, supported by the Regiment 'Hermann von Salza,' while its fuel and ammunition lasted. SS Lieutenant Colonel Paul Albert (Peter) Kausch led the final armored attack of the regiment and succeeded in checking the Soviet advance in the area. But it was a temporary victory. The French fell back from the Landwehr Canal, being unable to stem the Soviet thrusts, and crossed the area of

Kreuzberg towards the center of the city fighting. The French units took defence positions in the Belle Alliance Square, trying to block enemy access to the Chancellery and the bunker. Indeed, Fenet was moved on a chair from point to point in order to boost the morale of his men.

Dr. Krukenberg set up the last command post for the 'Nordland' Division in the Stadtmitte station of the subway *(U-Bahn)*, in a ruined trolley car under candlelight. SS First Lieutenant Babick, leader of the Reichstag defenders, set up his command post in the cellar of a house at the corner of Dorotheenstrasse and Hermann-Göring-Strasse, a few dozen meters north of the Brandenburg Gate. The cellar was a 23-square-meter air raid shelter. Babick had divided his men into groups of five to ten and he was convinced about the final victory, hoping that the reinforcements would include the Regiment 'Hermann von Salza' heavy tanks, most of which had been destroyed supporting the French volunteers. Sergeant Undermann's group was in the Ministry of the Interior, covering the southern end of the Moltke Bridge, connecting the two banks of the Spree. In a bid to keep the enemy from reaching the Reichstag 'fortress,' the defenders attempted to blow up the bridge up on 28 April. The bridge failed to collapse, however, and the Soviets managed to cross it a little after midnight. The battle then moved on to the Ministry of the Interior. The 'Nordland' fighters faced the Soviets in hand-to-hand combat, before falling back in the rubble around the Reichstag, where they caused many casualties to the attackers. The Soviets seized the Belle Alliance Square a little to the south; however, the French volunteers foiled enemy attempts to approach the Chancellery, firmly holding their

**SOVIET JUNIOR LIEUTENANT OF ARTILLERY**
*He wears a 1943 double breasted great coat and a pilotka side cap. Standard issue belt with map case. The Tokarev Model TT33 pistol 7.62 mm was a powerful weapon, despite its small caliber. The combination of power and light weight made it a rather violent weapon to shoot. (Illustration by Johnny Shumate / Historical Notes - Comments by Stelios Demiras)*

*Traudl Junge,
Hitler's secretary.*

positions in Wilhelmstrasse and Friedrichstrasse. The Soviets heavily pounded their positions with artillery and then renewed their ground assault on the morning of 29 April. The volunteers were renowned for masterly destroying enemy tanks in the ruined avenues of central Berlin. The determined French, with no artillery support, were blowing up one Soviet tank after another in front of their barricades using only *Panzerfaust* anti-tank launchers. The battle continued in the Gestapo headquarters building, 300 meters away from the Chancellery, at No. 8, Prinz Albertstrasse. The Soviets initially seized the building, but the French counterattacked and forced them to abandon it temporarily. One evening during the last days of April, the unit commander rewarded the defenders, who had shown exemplary courage, with medals. This ceremony was held under candlelight and signified "light winning over darkness," according to a 26-year old officer.

The last conference was held during the night of 29 April amidst reports that the Soviets were on the Wilhelmstrasse. It was attended by Hitler, Goebbels, Bormann, the Chief of the Army General Staff *(OKH)* Lieutenant General Hans Krebs, the Chief of the personnel department of the German Army Lieutenant General Wilhelm Burgdorf, the liaison diplomat with the Foreign Ministry Walther Hewel, Dönitz' Naval Liaison Officer Vice Admiral Hans-Erich Voss, Hitler's Luftwaffe adjutant Staff Colonel Nicolaus von Below and Lieutenant General Weidling. The latter made an appeal to the Führer to allow the troops defending the city to escape through the Soviet lines towards the west, given the fact that the Soviets were expected at the Chancellery the next day. Hitler, however, replied that such an attempt was impossible. After the conference, von Below left the bunker carrying a post-script to Hitler's will in order to deliver it to Field Marshal Keitel at Plön, in Schleswig-Holstein. He came up to the surface on the night of 29 to 30 April and caught up with the three aides in the Reichssportfeld. The four men managed to evade the Soviet troops and to move away from Berlin, but a few days later the Western Allies arrested them. The three copies of Hitler's will were discovered and were confiscated by the allied secret services.

Bormann assigned Hitler's Waffen SS adjutant, 27-year-old SS Major Otto Günsche, to arrange all necessary details after the Führer's death on the morning of 30 April. Adolf and Eva Hitler retired to Hitler's office after 1500. Günsche stood at the door so that no one would disturb them. Ten minutes later, it was all over. Dr. Stumpfegger examined the two corpses and verified their death. Then, Hitler's personal valet, Linge, and three officers of the guard carried Hitler's lifeless body to the Chancellery garden from the emergency exit. Bormann and SS Lieutenant Colonel Erich Kempka – Hitler's Driver – followed them carrying Eva's body. They deposited the remains 10 meters away from the entrance, doused them with gasoline, and set them on fire.

Hitler was dead. "The tension in the bunker, impossible to bear during the last 15 days, had subsided for a few hours at least," secretary Gerda Christian recounted. Chancellor Goebbels' first priority was to negotiate the capital's capitulation. After midnight, Krebs led a delegation across the battle zone to a Soviet command post. Talks lasted until the early hours of 1 May, but the enemy was uncompromising and insisted on unconditional surrender. Krebs returned to the bunker and his report cancelled all chances of talks about a truce. Christian recounts: "... we all knew that the Russians were closing in. We knew that breaking out from the siege, when and if it would come true, would be a rough experience."

Weidling left the bunker too, later, in order to go to the last command post at Vosstrasse, next to the Chancellery, to use a radio for a last attempt of getting in contact with the Soviets. At the same time, preparations began for putting the Goebbels family to death in the *Vorbunker* and the break out of those who chose not to commit suicide. At 1700, Magda Goebbels gave a chocolate with a sleeping tablet to each of her six children and put them to bed. When they fell asleep, they were administered poison, as two SS doctors, Stumpfegger and the dentist, Dr. Helmut Kuntz, were on standby in an adjacent room. Then, she looked for her husband and found him contemplating the first days of the rise of National Socialism. He was talking around a long conference table to his assistant Werner Naumann, the one-armed, 32-year-old Artur Axmann (the Hitler Youth Leader), Hitler's personal pilot, SS Lieutenant General Hans Baur, Hewel, Krebs and three or four others. Frau Goebbels sat down silently, sipping champagne and smoking. Her husband stopped talking after about an hour and then went up to the surface for a short walk in the Chancellery garden. He returned to his room at 18.15 and went down to the *Führerbunker* for

another time. He met his adjutant, SS Captain Günther Schwägermann and the local commander SS Major General Wilhelm Mohnke. Goebbels gave Schwägermann a signed photo of Hitler and said: "At least, you, the good people, will not have to carry our bodies on this long staircase." He then "wore his hat, his scarf and the long coat of his uniform. He took off his leather gloves slowly, taking great care for each finger. Then he presented his right arm to his wife, as a knight would do... They climbed the staircase towards the courtyard slowly but steadily, leaning one on the other," Mohnke recounts. They met an *RSD* officer on the landing, the only witness to what followed, and bypassed six petrol cans. Magda bit a cyanide capsule and fell down. Goebbels shot her at the back side of her head. He then straightened up, bit his own cyanide capsule, and shot himself in his right temple. The guard officer and Schwägermann poured gasoline over their bodies and set them ablaze.

*A photo of the Goebbels family with their six children, Helga, Hildegard, Helmut, Holdine, Hedwig, Heidrun, and Air Force Sergeant Major Harald Quandt, Magda's son from her previous marriage.*

*The southern corner of the Chancellery garden. From left: unfinished observation / ventilation post, the Führerbunker's exit and the second observation post.*

# Break-out

Almost 800 troops, 80 of them *RSD,* were left around the Chancellery. Major General Mohnke decided that the time had come to study the details of their break-out, given the fact that there were fewer than 20 members of Hitler's entourage left in the bunker. He divided the survivors into 10 groups and set a different route and time of departure for each group. Generals Krebs and Burgdorf, as well as Captain Schedle, had already decided to commit suicide. Finally, General Weidling agreed not to sign any surrender treaty before the morning of Wednesday, 2 May, giving them five hours during the night to carry out their break-out.

The break-out began at 2300. There were 20 people, including the four secretaries, in the first group, which was led by Mohnke. They crossed the underground garage and came up on the surface at Wilhelmstrasse, directly below the old Chancellery balcony. They walked through the subway tunnels, according to plan, and reached the Friedrichstrasse station, a few hundred meters further. They emerged into the street and headed north, along

Friedrichstrasse, towards the Weidendammer Bridge. Finally, they managed to cross the Spree River on a pedestrian bridge, next to the main bridge.

The other groups followed the subway and managed to reach Friedrichstrasse station, but, once they did, confusion reigned. Some became disoriented among the burning rubble of Berlin and the explosions of the Soviet artillery. Many succeeded in reaching the Weidendammer Bridge, but an anti-tank barrier and the heavy Soviet fire blocked its northern side. They had to retire to its southern end, where they soon encountered a group of German tanks. They gathered around them and moved again. This time they managed to cross the bridge with the tanks' support and they reached the northern banks of the Spree. When they reached Ziegelstrasse, however, a panzerfaust hit the leading tank. This violent explosion threw Bormann and Dr Stumpfegger to the ground and wounded Axmann, as they were closely behind it. Finally, they all fell back towards the Weidendammer Bridge; each individual now sought only to save himself.

Bormann, Stumpfegger, Axmann and others followed the railroad *(S-Bahn)* tracks. At the Lehrter station, Bormann and Stumpfegger decided to head to the east towards Invalidenstrasse. Axmann chose to head west, but he encountered a Soviet patrol and had to return to Lehrter station and follow his two comrades' escape route. Some time later, he caught up with them behind the bridge, where Invalidenstrasse crosses the railroad line. They were dead, lying on their backs. As Axmann saw no obvious wounds, he presumed they had been shot in the back. He continued on, escaped Berlin and

**SOVIET JUNIOR SERGEANT**
*He wears a plashch-palatka rain cape/shelter half. Beneath his overcoat, is wearing the traditional gymnastiorka shirt-tunic M1943, in khaki color and the M1935 sharovary trousers in same cloth and color. The helmet M1940 replaced the older one M1936 type. His decoration is a Stalingrad Medal. The Pistolet Pulemët Shpagina (machine pistol designed by Georgi Semënovich Shpagin). The PPSh-41 was rugged, simple, cheap, and effective. In addition to the 71-round drum, a 35-round box magazine was made for this weapon (as the curved magazine in this illustration). The PPSh submachine gun was as much a symbol of the Russian soldier as the MP38 was of the German. (Illustration by Johnny Shumate / Historical Notes - Comments by Stelios Demiras)*

reached the Bavarian Alps, where he hid for six months with Hitler Youth members, until he was arrested. Baur, the pilot, escaped carrying a small painting of Frederick the Great, a gift from Hitler. He lost one leg from a shell explosion and found himself in a Soviet hospital, without the painting, when he recovered. He was released in 1949. Admiral Voss, Linge the valet, Major Günsche and many others were captured and spent the next ten or more years in Soviet prisons. Kempka the driver, and secretaries Christian, Junge and Krüger reached the Western Allies. Others, such as SS Colonel Högel, an *RSD* member, were killed while trying to escape. The traces of yet others had been lost, such as Hitler's personal co-pilot, SS Colonel Georg Betz.

# The final confrontation

SS Major Rudolf Ternedde, commander of the battle group *(Kampfgruppe)* formed by the 'Norge' and 'Danmark' Regiments survivors, reported to Krukenberg at 2000 on 30 April. The divisional commander informed him about Hitler's death and ordered him to gather all survivors and to try to escape from the besieged capital. Only a few members of the 'Norge' and 'Danmark' Regiments actually managed to do so, however. Many troops found themselves trapped within the demolished buildings of central Berlin and took part in the defense of the Reichstag and other government buildings during these last hours.

The Reichstag's defenders did not abandon the building, even though Soviet guns had had it in their sights since the morning of 30 April. The battle raged in its interior until night fell. On the night of 30 April, First

Lieutenant Babick's underground command post provided shelter to 40 to 50 people troops and civilians seeking protection and waiting for the capitulation. Division 'Nordland' commenced its last attack on the night of 1 to 2 May. Swedish SS Captain Hans Pehrsson led his men along Friedrichstrasse, in an attempt to cross the Weidendammer Bridge. They did not manage to do so, however, and fell back. About 80 survivors found themselves at the Brandenburg Gate, where they surrendered.

The French volunteers counterattacked on the evening of 30 April and captured a Ukrainian NCO, who assured them that everything would end on 1 May. Lacking *Panzerfausts* the next day, the French were reduced to throwing hand grenades at the tanks that were closing in on them. The Soviets responded with flamethrowers and within minutes the unit command had been consumed by fire. The French fell back several dozen meters, abandoning the Gestapo building for good. Nevertheless, the battle continued unabated along Leipziger Strasse, Potsdammer Square, and in and around the Air Ministry. They remained firm in their positions when Soviet and German officers started talking about a truce on 2 May. Those who survived took refuge in the subway to avoid being captured. The battle for the French ended that same day, with the capture of the last 36 volunteers in the Potsdammer station. The French had managed to destroy about 60 Soviet tanks during the week they fought in Berlin.

Few were the men of the 'Charlemagne' formation who escaped the Soviets. The last Waffen SS Iron Crosses were awarded when these men contacted the 'Nordland' Division command post in the Chancellery for the last time: one to German First Lieutenant Weber, in the unit since it had been formed, and killed on 1 May; one to 22-year-old Sergeant Eugène Vaulot, killed on 2 May; and one to Sergeant Appolot, who had destroyed many enemy tanks. Appolot, a platoon leader at the divisional Battle School *(Kampfschule)*, was believed to have been killed by a sniper on 1 May; however, he managed to escape the Soviet ring and lived in France after the war. The fourth Iron Cross was awarded to Fenet. He and Appolot were the last unit survivors to have been awarded the highest medal. The seriously wounded Fenet was imprisoned in Soviet prisoner-of-war-camps and jails, after being hospitalized. He was condemned by a French court to 20 years imprisonment, but was released in 1949.

The foreign volunteers who fought in Berlin and returned to their countries were few. Ninety per cent of the bunker defenders who escaped survived. Of them, 90% was captured by the Soviets, but returned for a new life in post-war Germany after a 10-year imprisonment.

*Hitler and Eva Braun during happier times.*

# Notes

1. Members of the *Führer-Begleit-Brigade* that served in Hitler's headquarters wore a black cuff-band low on the left sleeve, bearing the inscription *Führerhauptquartier* sewn in silver thread.
2. Waffen-SS officers had an SS rank and a corresponding rank associated with the Wehrmacht, e.g.: SS-Brigadeführer and Generalmajor der Waffen-SS.
3. In the beginning of 1945, about 400 French grenadiers formed a construction battalion *(Baubataillon)*, which was used in fortifications. The rest (700 men) formed a signals platoon, an engineer platoon, a supply unit, a repair unit and the SS Grenadier Regiment 'Charlemagne' of two 1945 battalions (57th and 58th). They also formed a support battalion that would be composed of an anti-tank company, a tank-hunter company and an anti-aircraft company, provided the weapons became available.
4. The 1st Battalion of the 'Danmark' Regiment and the 1st Battalion of the 'Norge' Regiment had been detached from the 5th SS Panzer Division 'Wiking' in April – May 1945.
5. The organic panzer unit of the 'Nordland' Division, the 11th SS Panzer Regiment 'Hermann von Salza,' reached Berlin with a single PzKpfw V Panther (the only left after the battles of the summer of 1944), several *Sturmgeschütz III Ausf G* self-propelled guns and the heavy PzKpfw VI Ausf B *Königstiger* tanks of the 503rd SS Heavy Tank Battalion, which was the regiment's 2nd Battalion from the beginning of 1945.

# Death and ideology in Berlin 1945

World War II was coming to its end when the Western Allies' and the Soviet troops invaded Germany. The front contracted day by day, but the heart of National Socialism and of the German defense continued beating in Berlin, the capital of the Third Reich. The last act of the great ideological war would be played there, amidst the rubble of a destroyed city.

The Soviet Army reached the Oder River in Pomerania in March 1945. That was the last natural barrier before Berlin. The Third Reich's luck seemed to have been judged irrevocably, but the fight continued unabated and with more fanaticism than ever, both by the Germans and the Soviets. Both the communist and the National Socialist propaganda agreed on one basic point: this war was not just an armed conflict between states for economic or geopolitical interests; it was a bloody confrontation of two ideological systems, National Socialism and communism, (see note 1).

The outcome of the war added another, more immediate dimension to it. It was an operation of revenge and, accordingly, a looting frenzy for the Soviets and a survival effort and desperate resistance for the Germans. It was something more for the latter: the ostensible vindication of the long-lasting national socialistic rhetoric that capitalism and communism were fraternal systems and allied at heart. Putting this message into practice precisely expressed the political

*Recruiting poster for the French Waffen-SS Division 'Charlemagne.'*

AVEC TES CAMARADES EUROPÉENS
SOUS LE SIGNE ⚡⚡
TU VOINCOOS !

**SOVIET LIGHT MACHINE GUNNER**
*The quilted winter jacket* telogreika *in khaki color was highly efficient for field wear in the Russian winter and generally in the coldest climates. Note the M1935* sharovary *trousers of khaki cloth and the standard issue black leather boots. The helmet M1940 replaced the M1936 type distinguished by an appliqué metal crest. His light machine gun* Ruchnoi Pulemët Degtyarëva Pekhotny *(automatic weapon, Degtyarëv, infantry) better known as DP was the standard machine gun for the Soviet Army from 1928. A SVT-40 Tokarev bayonet (all purpose knife) has been slipped on the belt as well as a canteen. On the ground is a drum magazine case. (Illustration by Johnny Shumate / Historical Notes - Comments by Stelios Demiras)*

*German military training an elderly man, member of the* Volkssturm, **in the use** *of the* panzerfaust.

*"I expect each German to act out his duties to the end, to accept all sacrifices that have been or will be demanded. I expect each able-bodied person to give his body and his soul to the struggle... I expect from the city inhabitants to take up weapons, I expect the farmers to give bread to the soldiers and workers of this struggle.*

*I expect all women, young and old, to help this fight, as they have done until now with supreme fanaticism. In saying this, I address the German Youth in utter confidence... Europe will also win this battle, not Asia."*

**Adolf Hitler, 30 January 1945**

singularity of Germany. An independent observer would ask the following crucial questions: since National Socialism was a deliberate product of capitalism, according to the Communists, then why did it turn to fight against it? And since National Socialism was just a heresy of the socialist theories, according to the capitalists (the 'Western plutocrats'), then why did it use all its forces for the ideological and military crushing of a related system?

These theories are of very little value in the battlefield, as the prospect of death is more immediate, denuded of idealism and dressed in the horror of excess. The Soviet Army was advancing throughout the eastern front of Prussia and the atrocities committed were unsurpassed. During the last months of the war, the casualties suffered by Germany and the people of Eastern Europe, who were wounded, became refugees, or died, reached hundreds of thousands. These incidents were so devastating that they often brought on many simple citizens' extreme reactions, as well as the troops' moral confusion.

A wave of suicides swept Berlin, which sensed the enemy approaching. Especially among women, committing suicide was preferred to being at the mercy of the Soviets, the "sub-humans from the East." Moreover, the official Soviet military command advocated atrocities, not to mention individual cadres. Field Marshal Zhukov in his 6 March 1944 daily order mentioned: "Soviet soldier, here are the borders of cursed Germany, the country that caused you, your family and the Motherland to shed so much blood and tears. Behave in such a way that the entry of our troops should be written into the memory of not only the Germans of today, but of their most distant descendants." It is clear that the advancing Soviets faced the Germans as people not belonging to humanity. Consequently, all atrocities were allowed against such an enemy. It is typical that the Anglo-Saxon - Soviet coalition did not acknowledge the Germans their essential right of defending their country. There was no room for a territorial and geopolitical settlement. Germany had to be totally destroyed. The fact that the war was going in develop to that direction had been predicted many years before in a perceptive book by the German political theorist Carl Schmitt, titled *The Concept of the Political (Der Begriff des Politischen,* 1922): "Such kinds of war are by necessity intense and inhuman, because, they are transgressing the Political and they have to degrade the Enemy at the same time, referring to ethical and other categories, and to present him as an inhuman beast that must not be merely repulsed, but must be totally eliminated, which means that he is not merely an enemy that must be repulsed to his own borders" (see note 2).

As they watched an entire world collapse, that of National Socialist Germany, which had molded and reformed them, the German soldiers saw the situation from a unique point of view, blaming the failure of the Western states to grasp the real mission of National Socialism. Captain Schultis wrote a thrilling letter to one of his teachers, a liberal and an anti-Nazi: "We were wrong. Hitler was right, Koch was right, the ones who wanted to eliminate, to destroy, to annihilate were right... If we had not left any sign of life, they would not have been able to be here, they would not have been able to rape, to kill, to reduce us to slavery... have you seen the babies killed at Neuteich? And the women that were gang-raped 20 and 40 times in a night? And the 12-year-old girls whose abused bodies bled? No, you haven't seen anything. Nothing. You cannot see, because your incredible stupidity has become your conscience. And your stupidity is the West's stupidity that continues fighting us cheerfully, completely at ease with its conscience, since it fights against the Hitler regime that is unworthy of humanity...

"I am ready to spit when I listen to Radio London or Radio New York, which want to teach us the right thing and humanism. Churchill should come here, Roosevelt should come here... Nothing can be done anymore; we are a defeated people in the East. The Bolsheviks advance and we cannot do anything to stop them. Why, then, should we continue the fight? For Europe, for the others who, as God is my witness, write our errors with capital letters and those of the Russians with such small letters that they cannot even read them?

"No, total destruction is better. We should fall into the arms of the hell that advances from the east and say: do anything you want with us. But at least let us march with you against the West. We want to take revenge on

*The desperate German defense as the Soviets approached Berlin. This German soldier had just destroyed a Soviet T-34 tank with a* panzerfaust.

*"One fight, one will, one goal: Victory at any price!"*

*Recruiting poster for the Volkssturm: " For freedom and life!"*

*The Third Reich's military efforts ended in a tragic fight for survival: "Mothers, fight for your children!"*

Civilians, especially the youth, had been nurtured by the ideals of heroism, honorable death and the defense of the peoples' community *(Volksgemeinschaft)*. The population in Berlin had been fully mobilized thanks to the coordinated efforts of the local authorities, while the administration and Peoples' Militia *(Volkssturm)* units had been formed by October 1944.

The young members of the Junges Volk (10 to 14 years old) and Hitler Youth *(Hitlerjugend*; 14 to 18 years old) organizations showed particular enthusiasm. These children were everywhere: putting out fires caused by the merciless Allied bombings, rescuing and taking care of the wounded in *Volkssturm* units. Young children, boys and girls, were trained in shooting and in the use of the anti-tank *Panzerfaust*. They ran through the city, putting up signs and posters on the walls, calling the people to be alert. Their morale was high, their spirit uncompromising, and their faith fanatical. Huge signs were written all over the city: "Whoever believes in Hitler, believes in victory," "Berlin remains German," "Vienna will become German again," "We will never surrender," "The greatest time is in front of the rising sun".

The organizations' children continued parading in a half-destroyed city, boosting the morale of the rest of the population with their lavish courage. They sang about the inevitable death coming, however they still believed in Victory:

"A new people is rising, ready to attack
comrades, lift the banners higher
We feel our time is coming
the time of the new warriors
The dead heroes of the New Nation

those who refuse to realize that we do not fight only for ourselves, but for them too" (see note 3).

Most of the German troops, officers and the common people still had unusually high morale, even when the enemy reached Berlin's suburbs, a few kilometers from the center of the city. The structure and the character of the National Socialist regime helped this.

march in front of us with battered banners
and above us, our ancestor heroes
Germany, oh motherland,
now we are coming too."

The ring around Berlin tightened more during the first days of April. Goebbels' propaganda machine attempted to set the citizens' anxieties at ease. As they watched the precautionary fortification of the capital go up, with anti-tank ditches, barriers and minefields in the city's perimeter, they felt progressively more worried. Goebbels then leaked information to the press that the capital was secure, surrounded by an extensive network of defensive fortifications and incessantly called it 'Fortress Berlin' *(Festung Berlin)*. In reality, no more than the 9th Army and some Waffen-SS units were between the city and the Soviet forces.

Hitler was aware of the actual situation and took great care to stress the importance of the final battle on 15 April 1945, while addressing the defenders of Berlin in his daily order: "Soldiers of the Eastern Front! The hordes of our Bolshevik-Jewish enemy have gathered for the last attack. They want to destroy Germany, to eliminate its people. You, soldiers of the Eastern Front, have seen with your own eyes what they have in store for the German women and children. The elderly, the men and the babies are executed. Women and girls are abused and sent to whorehouses for troops. Whoever survives will be send to Siberia. (...)

"This time the enemy will face the ancient Asiatic destiny and will be decimated in front of the Reich's capital. Whoever does not fulfill his duty now is a traitor to the Nation. The regiments or divisions that will fall back from their positions should be ashamed, compared to the women and children that patiently endure the horror of the bombings.

"Berlin remains German, Vienna will remain German and Europe will never be Russian. Form a community under oath to defend not the abstract notion of motherland, but your land, your women, your children and with all these your future. The German

*German BAF 203 (r) BA-10M armored car from the Panzer Kompanie 'Berlin,' Berlin, April 1945. At the end of the Battle of Berlin every single captured vehicle was forced into action to defend the capital of the Third Reich. It was armed with a 45 mm gun and two 7.62 mm machine guns. Finished in a two-color scheme with Sand Yellow as the base and irregular stripes of Dark Green overpainted. (Illustration by Dimitris Hadoulas/Historical Notes by Stelios Demiras)*

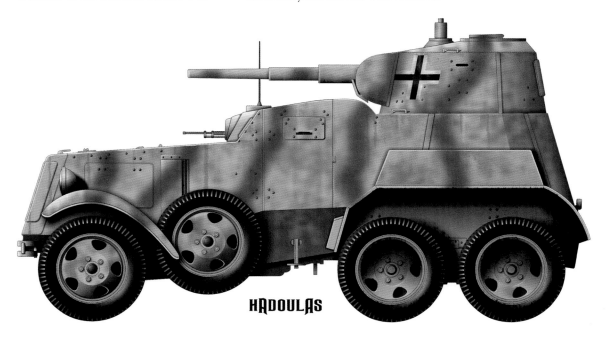

HADOULAS

*Members of the Hitler Youth march, armed with Panzerfaust and grenades.*

people have their eyes on you, soldiers of the Eastern Front, and hopes that your cohesion, your fanaticism and your weapons will be able to drown the Bolshevik attack in blood.

"The moment that fate removed the biggest criminal of all times [i.e., Roosevelt] from the face of the earth, the fates of war were predetermined. Adolf Hitler."

Hitler's words stressed some key notions in understanding the psychology of the German civilians during the last months of the war. There are direct and comprehensible references (saving the women and the children, Soviet atrocities), as well as ideological elements (fight against the Bolsheviks, defending the Reich and Europe). The consequences of defeat are described in all their horrible details so that the population will have a frame of mind for stubborn resistance. The Germans then were cornered and all their bridges were cut. Resistance and the war effort were not about holding defensive positions as a strategic move anymore, but about saving people, things and common beloved notions. Goebbels gave the word from the 'People's Observer' (*Völkischer Beobachter*, 17 April 1945 issue), the newspaper with the largest

circulation: "Each square meter of land that the enemy has to fight for, each Soviet armored vehicle that will be destroyed by a grenadier, a *Volkssturm* man or by a child in the Hitler Youth, today is worth a lot more than it was worth throughout the war. The word for today is: Clench your teeth. Fight like devils. Do not yield an inch of land. This decisive time demands the last and largest effort."

Military operations around Berlin were not going well for the German units. The Soviet armor showed up on the Reich's highways (*Autobahnen*). The last reserves for the Eastern Front, ten *Volkssturm* battalions, were armed and hastily sent off to an unequal confrontation, where certain death awaited them. These units were, mainly, composed of elderly people and children, ordinary civilians without any war experience, but especially armed with courage and self-denial. The ruined Berlin was full of signs and posters to bolster morale and called the German people to the last resistance.

The leaders of this resistance, naturally, were Hitler and Goebbels, the most important figures of the National Socialist Movement. Goebbels was in charge of the city's defense as the local governor (*Gauleiter*) of Berlin. At the same time, he was Reich Minister of Public Enlightenment and Propaganda and he gave ideological elements to the last defensive efforts, which was necessary to boost the Germans' morale. The city had been completely surrounded by 19 April. That same night, Goebbels addressed the German people for the last time on the radio. It was the eve of Hitler's birthday and Goebbels gave the customary message: "In this phase of the war, when for another time, probably the last one, the forces of hate and destruction attack from the

East and the West, I talk to you about the Führer in the same way I have been talking about him since 1933 to the German people, the night of the eve of 20 April.

"I can only tell you that this period, in all its dark grandeur, found its only worthy representative in the face of the Führer. Germany still survives thanks to him. We owe to him and him alone the fact that Europe and western civilization have not yet been misguided or fallen into the abyss opening in front of us. (...)

"We look up at him with hope and in firm belief. We follow him, proud and ready for the fight – soldiers and civilians, men, women, children, a determined people – to the death for his life and his honor. We want to preserve the German faith we have promised him and he has promised to us. Let us remain loyal to him, as he remains loyal to us.

"We call out to him 'Führer, order us, we obey,' because he knows and he can. May God give him power and health and protect him from all danger. We can take care of the rest. Germany is the land of loyalty. It will celebrate the greatest triumph in danger. When history will talk about these days it will never say that the people abandoned their leader or that the leader abandoned his people. And that is Victory."

Twenty April was an important day for National Socialist Germany. Goebbels had ordered a general decoration of all government buildings with flags. The swastika flew everywhere next to the signs: "Our walls broke, but no our hearts," "Berlin remains German," "The Führer is victory" and "We will never surrender." The party, state and army flags were hoisted for one last time. Hitler had been in the Chancellery bunker *(Reichskanzlei Bunker)* for a long time. Old friends and comrades-in-arms visited to wish him well. A Hitler-Jugend honor detachment was lined up in the Chancellery garden. Hitler came out of the bunker clearly exhausted. His gaze was hazy and he walked slightly unsteadily due to fatigue. Nevertheless, he greeted the youth members who spoke his name enthusiastically. For the children, Hitler was a mythical, almost superhuman figure, the man everybody referred to, and Germany's personification. The German leader congratulated the children for their courage and their loyalty and faith to him and they saluted him with their right hand extended, cheering "Heil Hitler!"

The Führer had already decided to remain in the capital until the final battle and the inevitable fall. Inspecting those children, no more than 15 years old, he finalized his decision to stay and die in Berlin. He, therefore, rejected some officials' suggestions to escape by airplane to Bavaria, which was still in German hands. All of Berlin was on fire and Hitler chose to put the seal on his political course in this way. Goebbels, with his wife and their six children, chose to do the same.

A new proclamation by Goebbels was put up on the walls on 22 April, a last appeal for resistance, containing threats and warnings for the luck German civilians would have in Soviet hands: "The city of Berlin shall be defended to the last man. Fight with unequaled fanaticism for your wives, your children, your mothers. We will resist. The Bolshevik great attack against the Reich capital is in full swing (...) The white flag means giving

*Elderly and younger men, who joined the Volkssturm.*

*Propaganda poster: "Germany's European mission." The idea of Europe was intensively cultivated by the National Socialists, especially during the last years of the war, and it came true in the battlefields with the Waffen-SS.*

up the war and shamefully losing one's life (...) The Bolsheviks wage a merciless war. Which of you wants his wife or his daughter to be raped? Which of you wants to be executed with a bullet in his head? Which of you wants to be led to Siberia? This time each of you knows your duty. Defenders of Berlin! Your mothers look up to you, your children and your wives look up to you. They have entrusted you with their lives (...) Fight for your city. Fight with unequaled fanaticism (...) Your *Gauleiter* is among you. He and his associates will remain with you. He seized this city with 200 men and now he will defend the Reich's capital by all means. This struggle for Berlin will be the light of national liberation for Germany. The capital cannot fall into the Bolsheviks' hands. National independence and social justice will reward your fight" (see note 4).

Troops that had been fighting at the front reached the destroyed city during the next days. Among them were various units of foreign volunteers in the Waffen-SS Division 'Nordland.' The division included Scandinavian and Flemish volunteers, as well as Lithuanian and Latvian battalions. There were also 300 French from the 'Charlemagne' Division and some Spanish. These international troops were the realization of the late National Socialistic vision for Europe: a Europe of the nations, a coalition against communism in the East. The European volunteers fought with a special fury and capability, as most were from countries under communist oppression or threat or were traditionally anti-communist. Among the hundreds of dead volunteers was Per Sorensen, the 'Danmark' Regiment commander. This regiment consisted of Danish fighters and they managed to save his dead body and move it to a cemetery close by. A German officer, Hermann, made a speech there: "We are here, at this grave to pay our respects to a brave Danish comrade, who distinguished himself as an exemplary officer and a commander of the 'Danmark' Regiment,' Per Sorensen. This moment "I have to express my people's thanks. He fought by their side faithfully with so many other Danish comrades. May you find peace here, in the bloodied heart of our city."

During his speech, most of the crowd became emotional and cried. The dead body was then hoisted down into the grave and rifles were fired three times over the uncovered grave. A woman threw some flowers, the men a handful of earth. The song "Ich hatte einen Kameraden" (I had a comrade-in-arms) completed this funeral (see note 5).

The battles inside and outside Berlin continued unabated. The idea of surrendering to the advancing Soviets seemed inconceivable, as everybody knew of the atrocities committed in the eastern German lands. The nihilistic slogan: "Enjoy war. Peace will be terrible" was popular among the German troops. Nevertheless, many deserted, especially civilians in *Volkssturm*, mostly towards the Americans in the west, where they hoped to be better treated. In private, Goebbels accused the generals for feebleness and some of the German people for cowardice: "We have not forced you, as we have not forced the German people. Why, then, did you cooperate with us? Your tender necks will be cut now. But when we fall, the earth will tremble" (see note 6).

The situation for the Berlin defenders was now hopeless. There were no reserves, re-supply was practically impossible, the communication and transport networks had been destroyed. The town was in flames from end to end, the makeshift hospitals were full of thousands of wounded, children as well as adults and elderly people. General Wenck's attack, aiming to relieve besieged Berlin, had failed and all attempts to save the Berlin pocket had been repulsed by 28 April.

The battle continued, violent as ever. French volunteers of the Division 'Charlemagne' threw themselves into the rubble against the Soviet positions, shouting: "Vive la France! Charlemagne! Heil Hitler," and passionately sang their songs in front of the Soviet armor:

"On your knees citizens and brothers
The shadow over us
The elect son of Victory
Napoleon, Napoleon."
A hand had written the following sign on a destroyed wall: "We are

dying so that Europe can live. Division 'Charlemagne.'" The Hitler Youth was fighting in another sector of the front through the ruins, with the few weapons it possessed, even with hand-grenades, knives and stones. At that point, the dead had reached hundreds of thousands. Berlin was collapsing in flames and the clash of weapons. It was the Wagnerian twilight of the Third Reich.

Hitler dictated his last will and testament during the early hours of 29 April, an evaluation of National Socialism and the last ideological manifesto: "More than thirty years have now passed since I, in 1914, made my modest contribution as a volunteer in the First World War that was forced upon the Reich.

"In these three decades I have been actuated solely by love and loyalty to my people... .

"It is untrue that I or anyone else in Germany wanted the war in 1939. It was desired and instigated exclusively by those international statesmen who were either of Jewish descent or worked for Jewish interests .. . Centuries will pass, but out of the

*German Gepanzerter Selbstfahrlafette für Sturmgeschütz 7.5 cm Kanone Ausf D (SdKfz 142) assault gun from the Infantry Division 'Ferdinand von Schill,' 12th Army, west of Berlin, April 1945. The StuG III superstructure was built on the successful hull of Pz III Ausf D. It was armed with a 7.5 cm KwK L/24 gun. It is finished in a three-color scheme with Sand Yellow as the base and over painted with irregular patches of Olive Green and Red Brown. The short, low-velocity 7.5 cm KwK L/24 gun has very poor armor-piercing performance, especially against the Russian tanks, but in the last days of the Battle of Berlin, every single tank or vehicle was forced into action to confront the Russian armor. (Illustration by Dimitris Hadoulas/Historical Notes by Stelios Demiras).*

ruins of our towns and monuments the hatred against those ultimately responsible, whom we have to thank for everything, international Jewry and its helpers, will grow... .

"I have also made it quite plain that, if the nations of Europe are again to be regarded as mere shares to be bought and sold by these international conspirators in money and finance, then that race, Jewry, which is the real criminal of this murderous struggle, will be saddled with the responsibility.

"I further left no one in doubt that this time not only would millions of children of Europe's Aryan peoples die of hunger, not only would millions of grown men suffer death, and not only hundreds of thousands of women and children be burnt and bombed to death in the towns, without the real criminal having to atone for this guilt, even if by more humane means.

"After six years of war, which in spite of all setbacks will go down one day in history as the most glorious and valiant demonstration of a nation's life purpose, I cannot forsake the city which is the capital of this Reich. As the forces are too small to make any further stand against the enemy attack at this place, and our resistance is gradually being weakened by men who are as deluded as they are lacking in initiative, I should like, by remaining in this town, to share my fate with those, the millions of others, who have also taken upon themselves to do so. Moreover, I do not wish to fall into the hands of an enemy who requires a new spectacle organized by the Jews for the amusement of their hysterical masses.

"I have decided therefore to remain in Berlin and there, of my own free will, to choose death at the moment when I believe the position of the Führer and Chancellor itself can no longer be held.

"I die with a happy heart, aware of the immeasurable deeds and achievements of our soldiers at the front, our women at home, the achievements of our farmers and workers and the work, unique in history, of our youth who bear my name... .

"From the sacrifice of our soldiers and from my own unity with them unto death, will in any case spring up in the history of Germany, the seed of a radiant renaissance of the National Socialist Movement and thus of the realization of a true community of nations.

"Many of the most courageous men and women have decided to unite their lives with mine; I have begged and finally ordered them not to do this, but to take part in the further battle of the Nation. I beg the heads of the Armies, the Navy, and the Air Force to strengthen by all possible means our soldiers' spirit of resistance in the National-Socialist sense, with special reference to the fact that also I myself, as founder and creator of this movement, have chosen death over cowardly abdication or even capitulation.

"May it, at some future time, become part of the code of honor of the German officer - as is already the case in our Navy - that the surrender of a district or of a town is impossible, and that, above all, the leaders here must march ahead as shining examples, faithfully fulfilling their duty unto death... .

"Above all, I charge the leaders of the nation and those under them to scrupulous observance of the laws of race and to merciless opposition to the universal poisoner of all peoples, international Jewry."

*Adolf Hitler*
*Given in Berlin, this 29th day*
*of April 1945. 4:00 a.m.*

The next day, 30 April, was Hitler's end; he committed suicide. Admiral Dönitz was appointed as his heir. Dönitz addressed the nation and the troops to the sound of Richard Wagner's "Funeral March" (*Trauermarsch*): "German men and women, soldiers of the armed forces. Our Führer, Adolf Hitler, has fallen. In the deepest sorrow and respect the German people bow. At an early date he had recognized the frightful danger of Bolshevism and dedicated his existence to this struggle. At the end of his struggle, of his unswerving straight road of life, stands this hero's death in the capital of the German Empire. His life has been one single service for Germany. His activity against the Bolshevik storm flood concerned not only Europe, but the entire civilized world (...)" It was simultaneously the last propaganda and a funeral oration for the entire National Socialist Third Reich.

# Notes

1. The first generation of post-war revisionist historians of Germany considered National Socialism (and European fascism in general) as an expected reaction of German society against the real threat of communism, which wanted to expand. See Ernst Nolte's works *Der europäische Bürgerkrieg 1917 – 1945: Nationalsozialismus und Bolschewismus,*

*The Minister of Public Enlightenment and Propaganda, Joseph Goebbels, inspecting Eastern Front troops.*

Hamburg 1987. A later and more perceptive approach regards National Socialism as a true and radical cultural revolution that turned against both communism and capitalism. See the persuasive views of Stanley Payne in his *A History of Fascism 1914-1945*). Also, J.Ellul, *Autopsy of Revolution,* New York, 1971 and E. Weber, *Revolution? Counterrevolution? What Revolution?* JCH 9:2 (2/1974), pp. 3-47.

2. Carl Schmitt, *The Concept of the Political (Der Begriff des Politischen).*

3. J. Thorwald, *La grande fuga,* Florence, 1964, p. 247.

4. Goebbels' last article was published in the 'Das Reich' newspaper on 22 April 1945, with the typical title *"Resistance at any cost" ("Widerstand um jeden Preis").*

5. Wilhelm Tieke, *Tragödie um die Treue: Kampf und Untergang des III Germanischen Panzerkorps.* Osnabrück, Munin Verlag, 1968, p. 217.

6. Fritzsche, Hans, and Hildegard Springer-Fritzsche, *Es sprach Hans Fritzsche,* Stuttgart, 1949, p. 31.

# The ideological weapons of the Red Army

## Soviet propaganda in the Battle of Berlin

The Soviet forces' advance along the entire Eastern Front favored Stalin's ulterior plans to seize the Third Reich capital first. It was a matter of prestige but, also, a matter of extending Soviet influence throughout central Europe. The mechanisms of the Soviet propaganda were mobilized in order to justify the merciless behavior of the Red Army and the need for the speeding up of the Berlin operation.

*"We are drinking water from our native Dnieper; we will drink from the Prut, Niemen and the Bug! [in black letters:] Let us cleanse Soviet soil of fascist filth!" 1943 poster by N. S. Ivanov.*

The official Soviet leadership propaganda towards the soldiers of the advancing Red Army during the last months of the war, when the strategic goal of seizing Berlin had been set, was in turning the Germans into demons and in justifying the atrocities against the non-combatant population. The contribution of a staff, with Ilya Ehrenburg, a man of letters and of Jewish descent, at its head, was decisive in defining the Soviet anti-German propaganda.

Ilya Ehrenburg, was for long known for his anti-German feelings and statements, long before the outbreak of the German-Soviet hostilities. Propaganda for mass reprisals against the invaders and, later, against the German population, intensified after 1942 and the checking of the German advance in the interior of the Soviet Union. Ehrenburg typically wrote in 1942: "Do not count days, do not count kilometers. Count only the number of Germans killed by you. Kill the German. That is your grandmother's request. Kill the German. That is your child's prayer. Kill the German. That is your motherland's loud request. Do not miss. Do not doubt. Kill."

During the late years of the war, when the Soviet advance towards the West had gradually begun (1943-45), Ehrenburg started inciting atrocities against the non-combatant German population, through newspaper articles, such as those published in *Krasnaya Zvezda*. Indeed, in one case he wrote that "the blond German bitch will have a very hard time," inducing rapes and other atrocities. He wrote a leaflet that was addressed to the Soviet troops in which he declared: "the Germans are not human beings... nothing gives us more pleasure than a heap of German corpses" (see note 1). Modern researches admit that Ehrenburg "always disliked the Germans and turned his old prejudices into basic positions of the Soviet propaganda as he was carried away by the maelstrom of the war" (see note 2). In another leaflet distributed to the Red Army, while the Soviets were approaching the town of Danzig in March 1945, an incitement, simple in its wording, but very clear as to the content, was included: "Soldiers of the Red Army! Kill the Germans. Kill all the Germans! Kill! Kill! Kill!" This leaflet was written by Ehrenburg, but was signed by Stalin and that was because in this way the Soviet troops could see that the authorization for inciting them into atrocities was high and any probable doubts would be swept away. There is evidence that the Soviet leadership did not always entirely approve of Ehrenburg's inciting atrocities against the noncombatant German population (see note 3). He was awarded the highest state awards, including the Order of Lenin and the Stalin Prize, for his significant contribution to the war effort and the raising of the morale of the troops.

The outcome of the official anti-German propaganda was horrible. There were incidents of gang-rapes, mass slaughter and executions, mutilations and abusing the dead in East Prussia, where the Soviets met non-combatant German civilians for the first time. In some cases, women who had been raped were murdered and put to the cross in public view in the areas of East Prussia. The atrocious tactics of the Russian Civil War (1918-1921) were revived in greater cruelty, since they were directed at a national enemy, the Germans, who had committed numerous atrocities themselves in the occupied Soviet territories during 1941-1943. German Army units that mounted a local counterattack in January 1945 were the ones who had located the unlucky victims on the cross. The Germans took photos and filmed the gruesome scene which was later shown all over the country, intensifying the will for resistance.

The Soviets launched one of the most violent artillery barrages in history on 16 April 1945. Field Marshal Zhukov's forces attacked the German positions in waves. A German machine-gunner who survived recounts: "We started firing against the mass of troops attacking us. There were no human beings in our firing field. They were a wall of attacking beasts trying to kill us. We ourselves were not humans anymore." In the meantime, the Soviet artillery continued its hammering, very often hitting friendly troops. Stalin was indifferent to the human cost, because he wanted to seize Berlin first, at any price. More than 30,000 Soviets died in the first three days, until 18 April, when the German lines were breached. The German casualties, on the other hand, were 10,000 men. What was important was that the road to Berlin had opened.

Joseph Stalin addressed the Red Army and the Allied troops on 21 April. He stressed the liberating character of the Soviet Army's actions, in reality preparing the Western Allies for the Soviet occupation of East Germany: "On behalf of the Soviet Government I address myself to you, commanders and men of the Red Army and of the armies of our Allies. The victorious armies of the Allied Powers who are waging a war of liberation in Europe have routed the German troops and have effected a junction in the territory of Germany. Our task, and our duty, is to deliver the finishing stroke at the enemy and compel him to lay down his arms and surrender unconditionally. This task, and this duty towards our people and towards all the freedom-loving peoples, will be carried out by the Red Army to the

*Propaganda poster of the Red Army praising the 1941-45 war.*

*Red Army troops storm the deserted capital of the Reich. In the foreground, the lifeless body of a German soldier.*

very end. I greet the valiant troops of our Allies who are now standing on German territory shoulder to shoulder with the Soviet troops, determined to perform their duty to the end." (see note 4).

The anti-German hate propaganda continued, and actually increased, during the last days of the war as the battle moved on to the Third Reich capital itself, where the most stubborn resistance was expected. On 1 May, a national holiday for the Soviet regime, Stalin added an official communiqué to his order of the day as supreme commander. He rebutted the charges of atrocities against non-combatant German people and rushed to show the might of the Red Army, of the Soviet state and, at the same time, of the communist political system. It was clear that the Soviets were preparing for the cold war confrontation with the Western parliamentary democracies. Having this in mind, the capture of Berlin would be tangible proof of the Soviet system's political health and of the achievements of communism. However, there seem to be some grains of worry, in the last paragraph of the text, about the atrocities the Red Army committed against non-combatant Germans and a foresight to reduce them.

In particular, Stalin mentioned: "Today our country is celebrating the First of May - the international festival of the working people (...) Today our victorious troops are routing the armed forces of the enemy in the heart of Germany, far beyond Berlin, on the River Elbe. In a short span of time Poland, Hungary, a large part of Czechoslovakia, a considerable part of Austria, and Vienna, the capital of Austria, were liberated (...) There can be no doubt that this circumstance signifies the end of Hitler Germany. The days of Hitler Germany are numbered (...) In their quest for a way out of their hopeless situation the Hitler adventurers resort to all sorts of tricks, even going to the extent of making advances to the Allies in an endeavour to sow discord in the Allied camp. This new chicanery of the Hitlerites is doomed to utter failure. It can only hasten the collapse of the German forces. Mendacious fascist propaganda is intimidating the inhabitants of Germany with absurd tales to the effect that the armies of the United Nations are out to exterminate the German people. It is not part of the task of the United Nations to exterminate the German people. The United Nations will extirpate fascism and German militarism, they will sternly punish the war criminals, and compel the Germans to make good the damage they have caused other countries. But the United Nations are not touching, and will not touch, the civilian population of Germany if they faithfully carry out the demands of the Allied military authorities.

"The brilliant victories the Soviet troops have achieved in the Great Patriotic War have revealed the titanic might of the Red Army and its high military skill. In the course of the war our motherland acquired a first-class seasoned army capable of defending the great Socialist gains of our people and of protecting the state interests of the Soviet Union. Despite the fact that for nearly four years the Soviet Union has been waging a war of unprecedented magnitude, calling for colossal expenditures, our Socialist economy is growing stronger and expanding, and the economy of the liberated districts, which was plundered and wrecked by the German invaders, is successfully and rapidly reviving (...)

"The World War, which was unleashed by the German imperialists, is drawing to a close. The collapse of Hitler Germany is a matter of the very near future. The Hitler bosses, who fancied themselves the rulers of the world, have now been left with a broken pitcher. The mortally wounded fascist beast is at its last gasp. The task now reduces itself to delivering the final stroke to this fascist beast.

"Men of the Red Army and Red Navy! The final assault on the Hitler lair is in progress. In the concluding battles set fresh examples of military skill and valour. Strike harder at the enemy, skilfully demolish his defences, pursue and surround the German aggressors, give them no respite until they cease resistance. While beyond the borders of your native land, be exceptionally vigilant! Continue to uphold the honour and dignity of the Soviet soldier!" (see note 5).

The Reichstag, the German Parliament, was seized on 2 May, after violent fighting in the suburbs and the center of the city. The Soviet flag was raised at its top, a clear symbolism of the communist political dominance in the heart of Europe. The Battle of Berlin was over, but the political gains for the Soviet Union were much greater, since it practically laid the foundations of its power in half of the European continent. The anti-German

propaganda emotions were still active, as is shown by a sign in the 1st Belorussian Front's headquarters: "Have you killed a German yet? If not, do so." The second wave of attack was the one that especially committed innumerable atrocities, breaches of the international law principals and the rules of fighting conduct. The Soviet troops behaved without any control, aided by the lack of discipline and the liquor quantities found in the German capital. Indeed, the Red Army was especially ruthless against civilians who had been mobilized by the National Socialist authorities for Berlin's final defense.

These men were organized in the Peoples' Militia (*Volkssturm*) units but the Soviets treated them as paramilitaries and, as a rule, executed them after they surrendered. Many Germans, though not enrolled in the *Volkssturm*, were considered to be members of secret resistance groups

*One of the most famous staged photos of World War II. The mounting of the Soviet flag on the Reichstag was not the actual capture of an emotionally charged moment, but the result of Ukrainian photographer Yevgeni Khaldei's ingenuity. This photo became part of History after having been suitably processed. An NCO actually wore two watches, indicating loot (one was 'rubbed out') and two of the soldiers were replaced by more European models. The 'replacements' were honored as national heroes and the real actors were told to forget about it.*

and were executed. The *NKVD* officials, the Red Army secret service, were in charge of liquidating all resistance groups left in Berlin, as well as of the subjection of the non-combatant population's morale.

However, the Soviet authorities inaugurated rapprochement politics to the Germans, for their own reasons, after the Third Reich's unconditional surrender. The plain Soviet troops, on the other hand, did not have any connection with these politics, naturally enough, and they continued looting, raping, committing atrocities and damages against the non-combatant German population for months after May 1945. Atrocities and acts of rape were even noted against Russian women, who had been imprisoned by the Germans and then liberated from the German concentration camps. These incidents gradually diminished by 1946, when the foundations for the post-war organization of the occupied German lands' administration were put into practice. The Soviet authorities' effort to eradicate the German people's faith in the National Socialist regime and in the German Armed Forces did not cease. They stressed the war crimes the Germans committed against Eastern Europe and the Jews, naturally not saying a word about their own war crimes.

# The political intentions of the Soviet authorities

The Soviet government had already begun changing its tactics of sterile anti-German propaganda by April 1945, when it realized that alienating the German population would not serve its post-war plans for consolidation of the Soviet control in the area. The Soviets had worked out a plan for political domination throughout Eastern Europe that would very soon materialize into forming the Warsaw Treaty of Friendship, Cooperation and Mutual Assistance.

Stalin addressed the citizens of the Soviet Union, praising the national factor of the Slavic resistance against German expansionism, on 9 May, the day that is celebrated since then as the Allied victory against National Socialism and the birth of united Europe. This position foreshadowed the formation of the eastern communist coalition, which practically was a coalition of the Slavic states for the control of Central and Eastern Europe, always under Russian suzerainty. Stalin's message was so worded as to also appeal to the German population, since it referred to the preservation of the political unity of the German state: "We now have full grounds for saying that the historic day of the final defeat of Germany, the day of our people's great victory over German imperialism, has arrived. The great sacrifices we have made for the freedom and independence of our country, the incalculable privation and suffering our people have endured during the war, our intense labours in the rear and at the front, laid at the altar of our motherland, have not been in vain; they have been crowned by complete victory over the enemy. The age-long struggle of the Slavonic peoples for their existence and independence has ended in victory over the German aggressors and German tyranny. Henceforth, the great banner of the freedom of the peoples and peace between the peoples will fly over Europe... The Soviet Union is triumphant, although it has no intention of either dismembering or destroying Germany. Comrades! Our Great Patriotic War has terminated in our complete victory. The period of war in Europe has closed. A period of peaceful development has been ushered in." (see note 6).

The Soviets hastened to take advantage of two factors concerning the German population's attitude. First, their desire to preserve an intact and united state and second, their resentment for, if not their hostility towards, the Western parliamentary democracies for their collaboration with communism. Their wish for the survival of a unified post-war German state was skillfully promoted by the Soviets, who talked about one German homeland, free from the Western powers' (Americans, British and French) occupation. Their bitterness for the West's position, which the German National Socialists thought realized the real Soviet danger and the Soviet imperialistic intentions, could be turned into support for a political régime like the communist one, that showed obvious similarities with the National Socialistic one, because both were totalitarian regimes. This tendency, which came about after 1945, developed into an intention to continue with a political attempt of organizing society based on totalitarian principles, this time with Soviet communism as a model. It was mainly a result of the intention for cooperation with the Soviet occupation authorities that some social groups in the newly formed East Germany showed.

Soviet propaganda during the Battle of Berlin, in April and May 1945, initially aimed at strengthening the fighting spirit of the Red Army troops, presenting the Germans as inhuman beasts that had to be eliminated. It gradually developed into trying to win over part of the defeated Germans, in order to make the establishment of the Soviet power in the occupied territories of eastern Germany easier. This new entity would, later, become independent - a satellite, obviously, of the USSR. Finally, some phrasings of the Soviet propaganda are considered as a prelude to the Cold War tactics that had already been inaugurated by the Soviets in 1945. The Soviets were building up the ideological characteristics of the eastern coalition by praising the communist political system and the solidarity of the Slavic people. Propaganda during the Battle of Berlin was especially successful and it served Stalin's plans for political control in East and Central Europe, as future developments showed.

*"Lets' go to Berlin!" 1944 poster by L. V. Golovanov.*

# Notes

1. Anatol Goldberg, Ilya Ehrenburg, p. 197
2. Anatol Goldberg, Ilya Ehrenburg, p. 193
3. Pravda, 14 April 1945 issue
4. J. V. Stalin, *On the Great Patriotic War of the Soviet Union*, Moscow, Foreign Languages Publishing House, p. 190
5. J. V. Stalin, *On the Great Patriotic War of the Soviet Union*, Moscow, Foreign Languages Publishing House, pp. 190-3
6. J. V. Stalin, *On the Great Patriotic War of the Soviet Union*, Moscow, Foreign Languages Publishing House, pp. 196-7
7. J. V. Stalin, *On the Great Patriotic War of the Soviet Union*, Moscow, Foreign Languages Publishing House, pp. 182-5

# SOVIET ORDER OF BATTLE FOR BERLIN

Units are listed as they were deployed from north to south on 16 April 1945.

**2nd Byelorussian Front (Marshal K. Rokossovsky)**
- 2nd Shock Army (Colonel General I. Fedyuninsky)
  - 108th Rifle Corps
  - 116th Rifle Corps
- 65th Army (Colonel General P. Batov)
  - 18th Rifle Corps
  - 46th Rifle Corps
  - 105th Rifle Corps
- 70th Army (Colonel General V. Popov)
  - 47th Rifle Corps
  - 96th Rifle Corps
  - 114th Rifle Corps
- 49th Army (Colonel General I. Grishin)
  - 70th Rifle Corps
  - 121th Rifle Corps
  - 191st Rifle Division
  - 200th Rifle Division
  - 330th Rifle Division
- 19th Army
  - 40th Guards Rifle Corps
  - 132nd Rifle Corps
  - 134th Rifle Corps
- 5th Guards Tank Army
  - 29th Tank Corps
  - 1st Tank Brigade
  - 4th Mechanized Brigade
- 4th Air Army (Colonel General K. Vershinin)
  - 4th Air Assault Corps
  - 5th Air Bomber Corps
  - 8th Air Fighter Corps

**1st Byelorussian Front (Marshal G. Zhukov)**
- 61st Army (Colonel General P. Belov)
  - 9th Guards Corps
  - 80th Rifle Corps
  - 89th Rifle Corps
- 1st Polish Army (Lieutenant General S. Poplawsky)
  - 1st Polish Infantry Division
  - 2nd Polish Infantry Division
  - 3rd Polish Infantry Division
  - 4th Polish Infantry Division
  - 6th Polish Infantry Division
  - 1st Polish Cavalry Brigade
  - 4th Polish Heavy Tank Brigade
  - 13th Polish SP Assault Artillery Brigade
- 47th Army (Lieutenant General F. Perkhorovich)
  - 77th Rifle Corps
  - 125th Rifle Corps
  - 129th Rifle corps

- 3rd Shock Army (Colonel General V. Kuznetsov)
  - 7th Rifle Corps (Major General V. Chistov/Colonel General Ya. Cherevichenko)
    - 146th Rifle Division
    - 265th Rifle Division
    - 364th Rifle Division
  - 12th Guards Rifle Corps (Lieutenant General A. Kazankin/Major General A. Filatov
    - 23rd Guards Rifle Division
    - 52nd Guards Rifle Division
    - 33rd Rifle Division
  - 79th Rifle Corps (Major General S. Perevertkin)
    - 150th Rifle Division
    - 171st Rifle Division
    - 207th Rifle Division
  - 9th Tank Corps (Lieutenant General I. Kirichenko)
    - 23rd Tank Brigade
    - 95th Tank Brigade
    - 108th Tank Brigade
- 5th Shock Army (Colonel General N. Berzarin)
  - 9th Rifle Corps (Lieutenant General I. Rosly)
    - 230th Rifle Division
    - 248th Rifle Division
    - 301st Rifle Division
  - 26th Guards Corps (Major General P. Firsov)
    - 89th Guards Rifle Division
    - 94th Guards Rifle Division
    - 266th Rifle Division
  - 32nd Rifle Corps (Lieutenant General D. Zherebin)
    - 60th Guards Rifle Division
    - 295th Rifle Division
    - 416th Rifle Division
    - 11th Tank Brigade
    - 67th Guards Tank Brigade
    - 220th Tank Brigade
- 8th Guards Army (Colonel General V. Chuikov)
  - 4th Guards Rifle Corps (Lieutenant Gen. V. Glazunov)
    - 35th Guards Rifle Division
    - 47th Guards Rifle Division
    - 57th Guards Rifle Division
  - 28th Guards Rifle Corps (Lieutenant General A. Ryzhov)
    - 39th Guards Rifle Division
    - 79th Guards Rifle Division
    - 88th Guards Rifle Division
  - 29th Guards Rifle Corps (Major General A. Shemenkov/Major General G. Khetagurov)
    - 27th Guards Rifle Division
    - 74th Guards Rifle Division
    - 82nd Guards Rifle Division
    - 7th Guards Tank Brigade

- 69th Army (Colonel General V. Kolpakchi)
  - 25th Rifle Corps
  - 61st Rifle Corps
  - 91st Rifle Corps
  - 117th Rifle Division
  - 283rd Rifle Division
  - 68th Tank Brigade
  - 12th SP Assault Artillery Brigade
- 33rd Army (Colonel General V.D. Tsvetaev)
  - 16th Rifle Corps
  - 38th Rifle Corps
  - 62nd Rifle Corps
  - 2nd Guards Cavalry Corps
  - 95th Rifle Division
- 16th Air Army (Colonel General S. Rudenko)
  - 6th Air Assault Corps
  - 9th Air Assault Corps
  - 3rd Air Bomber Corps
  - 6th Air Bomber Corps
  - 1st Guards Air Fighter Corps
  - 3rd Air Fighter Corps
  - 6th Air Fighter Corps
  - 13th Air fighter Corps
  - 1st Guards Air Fighter Division
  - 240th Air Fighter Division
  - 282nd Air Fighter Division
  - 286th Air Fighter Division
  - 2nd Guards Air Assault Division
  - 11th Guards Air Assault Division
  - 113th Air Bomber Division
  - 183rd Air Bomber Division
  - 188th Air Bomber Division
  - 221st Air Bomber Division
  - 9th Guards Air Night Bomber Division
  - 242nd Air Night Bomber Division
- 18th Air Army (Aviation Marshal A. Golovanov)
  - 1st Guards Air Bomber Corps
  - 2nd Air Bomber Corps
  - 3rd Air Bomber Corps
  - 4th Air Bomber Corps
  - 45th Air Bomber Division
  - 56th Air Fighter Division
- 1st Guards Tank Army (Colonel General M. Katukov)
  - 8th Guards Mechanized Corps (Major General I. Drëmov)
    - 19th Guards Mechanized Brigade
    - 20th Guards Mechanized Brigade
    - 21st Guards Mechanized Brigade
    - 1st Guards Tank Brigade
  - 11th Guards Tank Corps (Colonel A. Babadzhanyan)
    - 40th Guards Tank Brigade
    - 44th Guards Tank Brigade
    - 45th Guards Tank Brigade
    - 27th Guards Mechanized Brigade

- 11th Tank Corps (Major General I. Yushchuk)
  - 20th Tank Brigade
  - 36th Tank Brigade
  - 65th Tank Brigade
  - 12th Motorized Rifle Brigade
  - 64th Guards Tank Brigade
  - 19th SP Assault Artillery Brigade
- 2nd Guards Tank Army (Colonel General S. Bogdanov)
  - 1st Mechanized Corps (Lieutenant General S. Krivoshein)
  - 19th Mechanized Brigade
  - 35th Mechanized Brigade
  - 37th Mechanized Brigade
  - 219th Tank Brigade
  - 9th Guards Tank Corps (Major General N. Vedeneev)
    - 47th Guards Tank Brigade
    - 50th Guards Tank Brigade
    - 65th Guards Tank Brigade
    - 33rd Guards Mechanized Brigade
  - 12th Guards Tank Corps (Major General M. Telyakov/ Colonel A. Shevchenko/Major General M. Salminov)
    - 48th Guards Tank Brigade
    - 49th Guards Tank Brigade
    - 66th Guards Tank Brigade
    - 34th Guards Mechanized Brigade
- 3rd Army (Colonel General A. Gorbatov)
  - 35th Rifle Corps
  - 40th Rifle Corps
  - 41st Rifle Corps
  - 2nd Guards Cavalry Corps
  - 3rd Guards Cavalry Corps
  - 7th Guards Cavalry Corps
  - 3rd Guards Tank Corps
  - 8th Guards Tank Corps

**1st Ukrainian Front (Marshal I. Konev)**
- 3rd Guards Army (Colonel General V. Gordov)
  - 21st Rifle Corps
  - 76th Rifle Corps
  - 120th Rifle Corps
  - 389th Rifle Division
  - 25th Tank Corps
- 13th Army (Colonel General N. Pukhov)
  - 24th Rifle Corps
  - 27th Rifle Corps
  - 102nd Rifle Corps
- 5th Guards Army (Colonel General A. Zhadov)
  - 32nd Guards Rifle Corps
  - 33rd Guards Rifle Corps
  - 34th Guards Rifle Corps
  - 4th Guards Tank Corps
- 2nd Polish Army (Lieutenant General K. Swiersczewski)
  - 5th Polish Infantry Division
  - 7th Polish Infantry Division
  - 8th Polish Infantry Division

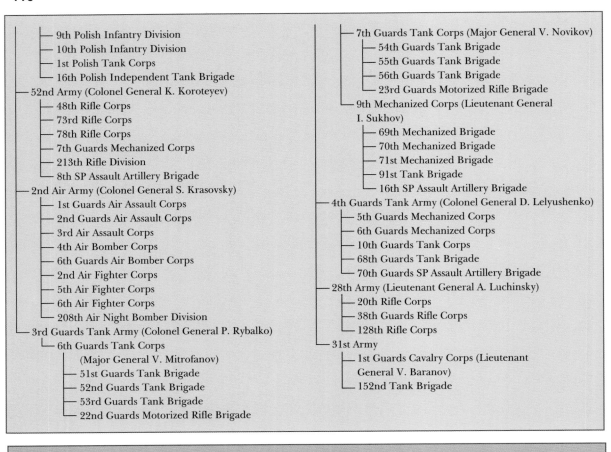

- 9th Polish Infantry Division
- 10th Polish Infantry Division
- 1st Polish Tank Corps
- 16th Polish Independent Tank Brigade
- 52nd Army (Colonel General K. Koroteyev)
  - 48th Rifle Corps
  - 73rd Rifle Corps
  - 78th Rifle Corps
  - 7th Guards Mechanized Corps
  - 213th Rifle Division
  - 8th SP Assault Artillery Brigade
- 2nd Air Army (Colonel General S. Krasovsky)
  - 1st Guards Air Assault Corps
  - 2nd Guards Air Assault Corps
  - 3rd Air Assault Corps
  - 4th Air Bomber Corps
  - 6th Guards Air Bomber Corps
  - 2nd Air Fighter Corps
  - 5th Air Fighter Corps
  - 6th Air Fighter Corps
  - 208th Air Night Bomber Division
- 3rd Guards Tank Army (Colonel General P. Rybalko)
  - 6th Guards Tank Corps
    (Major General V. Mitrofanov)
    - 51st Guards Tank Brigade
    - 52nd Guards Tank Brigade
    - 53rd Guards Tank Brigade
    - 22nd Guards Motorized Rifle Brigade

- 7th Guards Tank Corps (Major General V. Novikov)
  - 54th Guards Tank Brigade
  - 55th Guards Tank Brigade
  - 56th Guards Tank Brigade
  - 23rd Guards Motorized Rifle Brigade
- 9th Mechanized Corps (Lieutenant General I. Sukhov)
  - 69th Mechanized Brigade
  - 70th Mechanized Brigade
  - 71st Mechanized Brigade
  - 91st Tank Brigade
  - 16th SP Assault Artillery Brigade
- 4th Guards Tank Army (Colonel General D. Lelyushenko)
  - 5th Guards Mechanized Corps
  - 6th Guards Mechanized Corps
  - 10th Guards Tank Corps
  - 68th Guards Tank Brigade
  - 70th Guards SP Assault Artillery Brigade
- 28th Army (Lieutenant General A. Luchinsky)
  - 20th Rifle Corps
  - 38th Guards Rifle Corps
  - 128th Rifle Corps
- 31st Army
  - 1st Guards Cavalry Corps (Lieutenant General V. Baranov)
  - 152nd Tank Brigade

# GERMAN ORDER OF BATTLE FOR OPERATION BERLIN

Those units directly involved with the defense of Berlin are:

**OKW Reserve (Later allocated to the LVI Panzer Corps, 9th Army)**
- 18th Panzer Grenadier Division
- 30th Panzer Grenadier Regiment
- 51st Panzer Grenadier Regiment
- 118th Panzer Regiment (part)
- 18th Artillery Regiment

**Army Group 'Vistula' (Colonel General Gotthard Heinrici)**
- III SS 'Germanic' Panzer Corps (SS Lieutenant General Felix Steiner)
  (divisions later allocated to the 9th Army)
  - 11th SS 'Nordland' Panzer Grenadier Division (SS Major General Joachim Ziegler/SS Major General Dr Gustav Krukenberg)
  - 23rd SS 'Nederland' Panzer Grenadier Division (SS Major General Jürgen Wagner)
    (divisions later allocated to the 3rd Army)
  - 27th SS 'Langemarck' Grenadier Division
  - 28th SS 'Wallonien' Grenadier Division

3rd Panzer Army (General Hasso von Manteuffel)
- 'Swinemünde' Corps (Lieutenant General John Ansat)
  - 402nd Naval Division
  - 2nd Naval Division
- XXXII Corps (Lieutenant General Friedrich-August Schack)
  - 'Voigt' Infantry Division [Voigt Combat Group]
  - 281st Infantry Division
  - 549th Volksgrenadier Division
  - Stettin Garrison
- 'Oder' Corps (SS Lieutenant General Erich von dem Bach/General Walter Hörnlein)
  - 610th Infantry Division
  - 'Klossek' Infantry Division
- XLVI Panzer Corps (General Martin Gareis)
  - 547th Volksgrenadier Division
  - 1st Naval Division

9th Army (General Theodor Busse)
- 156th Infantry Division
- 541st Volksgrenadier Division
- 404th Volks Artillery Corps
- 406th Volks Artillery Corps
- 408th Volks Artillery Corps
- CI Corps (General Wilhelm Berlin/Lieutenant General Friedrich Sixt)
  - 5th Light Infantry Division
  - 606th Infantry Division
  - 309th 'Berlin' Infantry Division
  - 25th Panzer Grenadier Division
  - 111th SPG training Brigade
  - '1001 Nights' Combat Group
- LVI Panzer Corps (General Helmuth Weidling)
  - 9th Fallschirmjäger Division (General Bruno Bräuer/Colonel Harry Hermann)
  - 20th Panzer Grenadier Division (Colonel/Major General Georg Scholze)
  - 'Müncheberg' Panzer Division (Major General Werner Mummert)
- XI SS Panzer Corps (SS General Matthias Kleinheisterkamp)
  - 303rd 'Döberitz' Infantry Division
  - 169th Infantry Division
  - 712th Infantry Division
  - 'Kurmark' Panzer Grenadier Division
  - Frankfurt an der Oder Garrison (Colonel/Major General Ernst Biehler)
- V SS Mountain Corps (SS General Friedrich Jeckeln)
  - 286th Infantry Division
  - 32nd SS '30 Januar' Volksgrenadier Division
  - 391st Security Division

Army Group Center (Field Marshall Ferdinand Schörner)
- 4th Panzer Army (General Fritz-Hubert Gräser) (later transferred to the 9th Army)
  - V Corps (Lieutenant General Eduard Wagner)
    - 35th SS Police Grenadier Division
    - 36th SS Grenadier Division
    - 275th Infantry Division
    - 342nd Infantry Division
    - 21st Panzer Division
- 12th Army (General Walther Wenck)
  - XX Corps (General Karl-Erik Köhler)
    - 'Theodor Körner' RAD Division
    - 'Ulrich von Hutten' Infantry Division
    - 'Ferdinand von Schill' Infantry Division
    - 'Scharnhorst' Infantry Division
  - XXXIX Panzer Corps (Lieutenant General Karl Arndt) (12-21 April 1945 under *OKW* with the following structure)
    - 'Clausewitz' Panzer Division
    - 'Schlageter' RAD Division
    - 84th Infantry Division (21-26 April under 12th Army with the following structure)
    - 'Clausewitz' panzer Division
    - 84th Infantry Division
    - 'Hamburg' Reserve Infantry Division
    - 'Meyer' Infantry Division
  - XXXXI Panzer Corps (Lieutenant General Rudolf Holste)
    - – 'von Hake' Infantry Division
    - 199th Infantry Division
    - 'V-Weapons' Infantry Division
    - 1st HJ Tank Detstroyer Brigade 'Hermann Göring' Jagdpanzer Brigade
  - XXXXVIII Panzer Corps (General Maximillian Reichsherr von Edelsheim)
    - 14th Flak Division
    - 'Leipzig' Battle Group
    - 'Halle' Battle Group

**Ungrouped Formations**
'Friedrich Ludwig Jahn' RAD Division (Colonel Gerhard Klein/Colonel Franz Weller)
'Potsdam' Infantry Division (Colonel Erich Lorenz)

*Note: The tables on the Soviet and German Orders of Battle are based on the original, Tony Le Tissier's book I.*

# The opposing commanders

## General Gotthard Heinrici

Gotthard Heinrici was born on Christmas Day, 1886, in Gumbinnen, East Prussia. He joined the German Army when he was 20 years old and served both in the Western and Eastern Fronts during World War I, gaining much experience. He preferred the military profession to the financial uncertainty of destroyed Germany during the Interwar years and remained in the Army as one of its 100,000 Reichswehr cadres, becoming a Major General in 1936. Heinrici commanded the XII Corps when the Wehrmacht launched its lightning attack in the West in May 1940 and managed to achieve a breakthrough in a sector of the Maginot Line. In June 1941 he took part in the much more ambitious Operation 'Barbarossa,' as Commanding General XLIII Corps in General Guderian's Panzer Group 2 (*Panzergruppe*). He received the Knight's Cross for his services in the campaign. He was promoted to General in January 1942 and took up command of the 4th Army. He showed exceptional ingenuity and skill in defensive battles during the next two years by successfully repulsing attacks

*General Gotthard Heinrici*

of superior Soviet forces and was awarded the Oakleaves in November 1943 for it. He was made 1st Panzer Army Commander in August 1944 and succeeded Himmler as Commander-in-Chief of the unlucky Army Group Vistula in March 1945, having already been awarded the Swords on the Knight's Cross. His unfeasible mission was to defend the Oder and Berlin fronts. While defeat seemed bleaker than ever those days, Heinrici was relieved of his duties on 28 April 1945 but could not deliver his command formally to General Kurt von Tippelskirch due to the circumstances. He died on 13 December 1971.

## General Walter Wenck

Walter Wenck was born in 1900. From 1939 to 1942 he was Chief of Operations for the First Panzer Division. In 1942, he was an instructor for the War Academy, Chief of Staff for the LVII Corps, Chief of Staff for the Third Romanian Army fighting on the Eastern Front and Chief of Staff of Army Detachment Hollidt which conducted operations on the Lower Don when the encircled 6th Army was eliminated in the Stalingrad pocket. Wenck performed highly in all these duties and, at the age of 42, became the youngest general of the German Army. He continued being assigned to staff

positions (in the reformed 6th Army in 1943 and in the 1st Panzer Army in 1943-44). In 1944, he went still higher when he became Chief of Staff of Army Group South Ukraine and in the end of the same year he became Quartermaster General. The most dramatic part of his career began in March 1945 when he was recalled to duty from the medical leave he had taken, due to a car accident he had the month before. He was posted as commander of the 12th Army and tried to open a corridor to Berlin from the west but failed in doing so. He was captured by the Americans and remained in jail until 1947. He died in 1982.

*General Walter Wenck*

## General Theodor Busse

Theodor Busse was born in Frankfurt an der Oder in 1897 and joined the Kaiser's army as officer cader in 1915. When World War II began, Busse was a Lieutenant Colonel in the *OKH* staff, while later he became Chief of Operations (Ia) in the 11th Army staff (1940-42), Chief of Operations of Army Group Don (1942) and Chief of Staff of Army Group South (1943-44). On 7 July 1944 he replaced the most capable Hellmuth Priess as General Officer Commanding 121st Infantry Division, the beginning of his sudden rise to

## The opposing commanders

the highest echelons. He was brother-in-law and close friend to Lieutenant General Wilhelm Burgdorf, who was a fanatic follower of the National Socialist Party and the Chief of the Personnel Department of the German Army, which helped him in being promoted to the command of I Corps, though his command experience as a divisional commander was only two months! His personal connections were key to him taking command of the 9th Army on 9 January 1945. His Army was on the path of the Soviet steamroller, which smashed the German divisions fighting west of the Oder and Neisse Rivers. Busse managed to escape to the west and surrender to the Americans, though most of his Army was destroyed or captured by the Soviets. He died in Wallerstein in 1986.

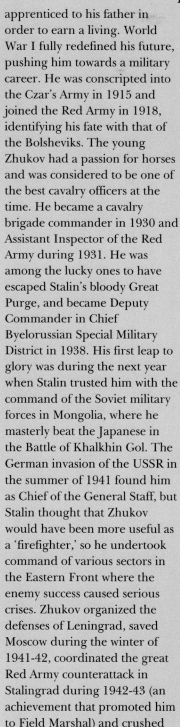

*General Theodor Busse*

# Field Marshal Georgy Konstantinovich Zhukov

Georgy Konstantinovich Zhukov was born on 2 December 1896 in a village of the Kaluga province, close to Moscow. He was the son of a poor cobbler and had to be

apprenticed to his father in order to earn a living. World War I fully redefined his future, pushing him towards a military career. He was conscripted into the Czar's Army in 1915 and joined the Red Army in 1918, identifying his fate with that of the Bolsheviks. The young Zhukov had a passion for horses and was considered to be one of the best cavalry officers at the time. He became a cavalry brigade commander in 1930 and Assistant Inspector of the Red Army during 1931. He was among the lucky ones to have escaped Stalin's bloody Great Purge, and became Deputy Commander in Chief Byelorussian Special Military District in 1938. His first leap to glory was during the next year when Stalin trusted him with the command of the Soviet military forces in Mongolia, where he masterly beat the Japanese in the Battle of Khalkhin Gol. The German invasion of the USSR in the summer of 1941 found him as Chief of the General Staff, but Stalin thought that Zhukov would have been more useful as a 'firefighter,' so he undertook command of various sectors in the Eastern Front where the enemy success caused serious crises. Zhukov organized the defenses of Leningrad, saved Moscow during the winter of 1941-42, coordinated the great Red Army counterattack in Stalingrad during 1942-43 (an achievement that promoted him to Field Marshal) and crushed

*Field Marshal Georgy Konstantinovich Zhukov*

the panzers' force for good in the Battle of Kursk (1943). Zhukov was the only Soviet soldier who was awarded the Hero of the Soviet Union medal four times, although at times he committed serious tactical errors that cost his troops dearly, such as Operation 'Mars' in 1943 and the Seelow Heights battles in 1945. Postwar he became Minister of Defense (1955) and a member of the Communist Party Central Committee in 1957, but was expelled from all public positions he held in October of the same year, because his prestige was envied by the party establishment. He died on 18 June 1974.

# Field Marshal Ivan Stepanovich Konev

Ivan Stepanovich Konev was born into a peasant family on 28 December 1897. He worked as a lumberjack before becoming an officer in the Czarist Army during World War I. He joined the Red Army in 1918 and in the next years he served as a political commissar in various armored trains. Thanks to his devotion to the Party his professional career was rapid: he was regimental commander in 1932, a divisional commander in

# The opposing commanders

1934 and commander of the 2nd Red Banner Army in the Far East in 1938. Stalin assigned him to the command of the 19th Army in the Moscow sector during the hard winter of 1941. Konev showed such virtues, that was nicknamed 'the general who never retreated' and soon took command of the Kalinin Front. His star began to shine from the time of the Battle of Kursk, where he crushed the German panzer divisions in the greatest tank battle of History with his timely intervention, while he was commander of the reserve Steppe Front. He then received the field marshal baton after the elimination of the German Korsun Pocket in February 1944. Konev is associated with the greatest victories of Soviet arms in the last two years of the war, when he was commander of the 1st Ukrainian Front, decisively contributing to the liberation of Ukraine, the capture of Poland and the fall of Berlin. Postwar, he was head of the Soviet occupation forces in Austria (1945-46), Commander of the Ground Forces and First Deputy Minister of Defense (1946-50), Inspector-General of the Soviet Army (1950-51), Commander-in-Chief of the Armed Forces of the Warsaw Pact (1956-60), Commander-in-Chief of the

*Field Marshal Ivan Stepanovich Konev*

Soviet occupation forces in East Germany (1961-62), where he built the Berlin Wall and Inspector-General of the Defense Ministry in 1962. He was a cultured man, despite his humble origins. It is said that he always carried Tolstoy's *War and Peace* and Livy's *History of Rome* with him. Konev died in 1973 and was buried in the Kremlin.

## General Vasily Ivanovich Chuikov

Vasily Ivanovich Chuikov was born on 12 February 1900 in the Tula Province. He would have followed his family in working in the fields, but the Russian Revolution pushed him into joining the Red Guards in 1917. He took part in many battles of the Civil War in the Ural Mountains and Siberia and, by the end of that fratricidal conflict, he was a colonel. He decided to follow a military career, studied in the Frunze Military Academy and then served in various positions in the Soviet Far East, including as an attaché in China in 1925 and 1927-29. He returned to Moscow in 1932-35 and attended the Academy of Mechanization and Motorization, a qualification that allowed him to take command of a mechanized brigade in 1936. Two years later, he was given command of the 5th Corps and he took part in the capture of

*General Vasily Ivanovich Chuikov*

Eastern Poland in 1939 as head of the 4nd Army. His 9th Army was mauled by the Finns at Suomussalmi in November of the same year, but Chuikov was promoted to Lieutenant General in June 1940 and was sent again to the Soviet embassy in China a little later. It seemed that his career was not going well, until Stalin recalled him to active service and assigned him to command the 62nd Army that was defending Stalingrad. His steadfast defense was monumental and he saved the city. His Army was honorarily re-designated as the 8th Guards Army in April 1943. The epic battles for the liberation of the USSR, as well as the capture of Poland and Berlin, followed, where Chuikov's troops were in the frontline. Chuikov accepted the surrender of the remnants of the Garrison of Berlin on 2 May 1945 and he was Commander-in-Chief of the Group of Soviet Forces in Germany in 1949-53. He was promoted to Field Marshal in 1955, was the Commander-in-Chief of the Ground Forces and First Deputy Minister of Defense from 1961-1972 and Chief of the Civil Defense. He died in March 1982.

# Lesser-known details

● On the day Stalin called a meeting of the highest Soviet military leadership - 1 April - in the Kremlin to plan the Battle of Berlin, he answered to a message of Eisenhower that informed him of the planned Allied operations. He reassured the American general that "Berlin has now lost its strategic significance" and that the Soviet command would only engage secondary forces against it. He also mentioned that the Red Army planned to give the next major blow to the south in the second half of May 1945, in order to meet the Western Allied forces. An apt comment of British historian Antony Beevor: "This was the largest April Fool's Day lie in modern history."

● The Berlin telegraph service ceased functioning on 27 April 1945. The last telegram was received from Tokyo: "Good luck to you all."

● A prisoner of war captured close to Küstrin on the eve of the great Soviet offensive in the Oder – Neisse Front told the Germans that the Red Army's assault would start on 16 April with a massive artillery barrage and the mass use of new heavy-type tanks. He also told them that the Soviet troops were ordered to wash themselves and to be shaved daily in order to "give the impression, from now on, of civilized people."

● One of the great fears of

the Soviets, as they were approaching Berlin, was the possibility of the German Army using chemical weapons against them. There were reports coming from Sweden that quantities of the nerve gases Sarin and Tabun, produced in the Spandau suburb of Berlin, were delivered to the German troops. The Soviet command worried that these 'weapons of despair' were going to be used and ordered all its troops to wear the gas mask four hours a day and to sleep wearing them for at least one night, in

*One of the 1,500 Soviet armored vehicles that swept through the German capital in the spring of 1945 is moving on one of its roads. To the right, an inscription that ironically reflected the desperate attempt to distort reality by the Goebbels propaganda mechanism: "Berlin remains German."*

order to familiarize themselves with the danger.

● The 16/69 Volkssturm Battalion at Briesen, on the Oder front, had only 113 men, of which 32 were constructing defense works in the rear and 14 were sick or wounded. The unit had three types of machine-guns (including Russian ones), one flamethrower that didn't work,

three Spanish pistols and 228 rifles of six different types.

● The 1st Belorussian and the 1st Ukrainian Fronts fired 1,236,000 rounds of a total weight of 98,000 tons against the German positions during the 16 April artillery barrage. That was the equivalent of 2,450 railway wagon loads.

● Stalin had another serious reason for wanting to seize Berlin the soonest possible, apart from prestige. The Soviet secret services had learned that the Kaiser Wilhelm Institute of Physics in Dahlem, a southwestern

suburb of Berlin, was the center of the German 'nuclear research.' Its installations were in a bunker that was inside coated with lead and it possessed a cyclotron that could produce voltage of 1,500,000 Volts. Seven tons of uranium oxide were stored in it, valuable material for the Soviet scientists, who were trying to build the USSR atomic bomb in a top secret program called Operation 'Borodino.'

● Undoubtedly, the hero of the Battle for the Seelow Heights for the German side was Sergeant Major Gernhert, an assault gun commander, who destroyed seven Soviet tanks on 16 April. On the next day his personal record reached 44.

● Thirty five Luftwaffe pilots of the 'Leonidas' Squadron (2./II/ KG200) flew a suicide mission in a desperate attempt to stem the Soviet attack in April 1945. Along with their aircraft and the bombs they were carrying, they hit the Oder bridges, on which enemy troops were moving to the west.

● Training the Soviet recruits was not good in 1945. Twenty three soldiers were killed and another 67 wounded in a division during one month, due to incorrect use of their light machine-guns.

● During the first two days of Zhukov's attack (16 and 17 April) the German 9th Army reported that it destroyed 211 and 106 Soviet tanks respectively, while the 4th Panzer Army, operating in the Neisse front, 93 and 140 tanks.

● The 1st Belorussian Front engineers constructed 25 bridges and used 40 pontoon bridges on the Oder River and the 1st Ukrainian Front had used 2,440 wooden engineer boats, 750 assault bridges and more than 1,000 bridge parts for the forced crossing of the Neisse River.

● The honorary position of the military commandant of a captured enemy city was given by right to the commander of the first unit to enter it. This was according to Russian military tradition, as it had been formed since the time of General Suvorov's campaigns. Accordingly, General Berzarin, commander of the 5th Shock Army, became the first Military Commandant of Berlin. This officer was killed on 16 June 1945 under obscure conditions. According

*Soviet assault detachment, supported by a tank, trying to clear the rubble of a building from its German defenders.*

# Lesser-known details

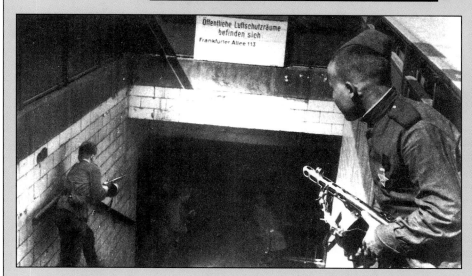

*Soviet soldiers storming the Berlin U-Bahn.*

to the official version of the events, it was a traffic accident. He was driving a motorcycle while drunk.

● One of the last victims of the Battle of Berlin was Ernst Himmler, the *Reichsführer-SS*, Heinrich Himmler's, brother. He was working as a technician in the German Radio studios and was killed at the Charlotten Bridge the night of 1 May, while trying to escape the city with other non-combatants.

● The Red Army fired 1,800,000 artillery rounds against Berlin between 21 April and 2 May 1945, the time of the Berlin siege.

● The rapes of German women committed during the Red Army's advance west of the Oder must have been numerous, considering that 130,000 women sought medical assistance these days in hospitals. It is estimated that the number of rape victims was higher and many cases were reported about German women of all ages who had been murdered by the Soviets, or who committed suicide out of shame.

● Each Soviet soldier taking part in the battle for the capture of Berlin was allowed, by the Red Army command, to bring back home 'war loot of 15 kg weight,' while officers were allowed 30 kg.

● A day before the Soviet attack in the Oder, General Heinrici asked for permission to move his headquarters to a new location, west of Berlin, even further behind Hitler's headquarters. Hitler, naturally enough, rejected that puzzling request.

● When Hitler woke up on 29 April he was informed that Benito Mussolini and his lover, Clara Petacci, had been dragged by Italian anti-fascist partisans in the central square of Milan, where they had been executed and hung upside down on meat hooks. This led the German dictator to his decision to commit suicide soon, so that his faithful colleagues would have the time needed to cremate his body, in order for it not to fall into enemy hands.

● Six Soviet armies (3rd Shock, 8th Guards, 1st, 2nd, 3rd and 4th Guards Tank) were placed as occupation forces in Germany right after the end of the war due to the bravery they had shown during the Battle of Berlin. Almost 45 years later, these same formations that had seized the Third Reich capital were among the last to withdraw from East Germany after the collapse of the Soviet Union and the Warsaw Pact disbanding.

# Photofile of the Battle of Berlin

*Bronze eagle from the Reichstag. Sold by a Soviet officer to a British colleague in 1946. Today it is displayed in the Imperial War Museum, London. Note the bullet holes from the battle of the Reichstag.*

*A realistic representation of the destroyed Reichstag in a diorama, at the Museum of the Great Patriotic War, Moscow.*

*Thousands of war booty items from the National Socialist regime came into the hands of the Soviets after the fall of Berlin. Hundreds of flags and banners were moved to Moscow, where they were displayed in the great military parade organized to celebrate the victory against National Socialism. Today they are displayed at the Museum of the Great Patriotic War, Moscow.*

*Another item from Berlin which today is displayed at the Museum of the Great Patriotic War, Moscow.*

*German VG-1 7.92 mm semi-automatic rifle of the Peoples' Militia (Volkssturm). Volkssturm's initial armament was from war booty; later, however, from January 1945, it was equipped with the VG-1. Its production was inexpensive and easy, as was its use. About 10,000 VG-1s were built until the end of the war.*

*A souvenir from a German border post, today displayed at the Museum of the Great Patriotic War, Moscow.*

*The memories of the victory against National Socialism and about the 'Great Patriotic War,' Soviet Union's participation in WW II, are kept alive in Russia to our days. Indeed, there are tens of museums about the war and the largest and most complete is the Museum of the Great Patriotic War in Moscow.*

*Tunic from a Peoples' Militia (Volkssturm)* **Major.** *The Volkssturm was formed in September 1944 by Hitler's decision and was composed of men aged 16 to 60. They bore the Volkssturm armband on their left arm.*

*Soviet ISU-122 122 mm self-propelled gun. The great shortage in 152 mm ML-20S guns forced the Soviets to mount the 122 mm A-19 gun in ISU-152s, turning them into ISU-122s. The first ISU-122s came off the production line in December 1943, at the same time as the ISU-152s. By June 1945, the total production of the ISU-152 and the ISU-122 had reached 4,000 tanks. Although the ISU-122 122 mm self-propelled gun was generally considered a very efficient long-range tank destroyer, in the Battle of Berlin it was used to destroy fortified positions at close range.*

*The typical Soviet T-34/85 tank armed with an 85 mm gun. It bears the characteristic white stripes that were the air recognition signs all Soviet tanks had from April 1945 to the Battle of Berlin. These stripes made it easy for the Allied aircraft to recognize the Soviet tanks as such and, thus, to avoid opening fire against them.*

*Berlin's anti-aircraft defence was based on hundreds of weapons of all calibres. Here is the typical German 88 mm gun. It also played an anti-tank role in the Battle of Berlin.*

*Soviet ISU-152 152 mm self-propelled gun. Essentially, it was the 152 mm ML-20S gun (which was also used in the earlier SU-152) mounted on the modified hull of the JS-2 (Joseph Stalin 2) heavy tank. The ISU-152 was externally similar to the SU-152. It was used to destroy fortified positions from a close range, like the ISU-122.*

# Bibliography

Armstrong, Richard N., *Red Army Tank Commanders: The Armored Guards*, Atglen, Pennsylvania, Schiffer, 1994.

Baird, Jay W, *The Mythical World of Nazi War Propaganda 1939-1945*, Minneapolis, University of Minnesota Press, 1974.

Balfour, Michael L. G., *Propaganda in War 1939-1945: Organisations, Policies and Publics in Britain and Germany*, London, Routledge, 1979.

Bahm, Karl F., *Berlin 1945: The Final Reckoning*, St. Paul, Minnesota, MBI Publishing, 2001.

Beevor, Antony, *Berlin: The Downfall, 1945*, London, Penguin, 2003.

Bullock, Alan, *Hitler: A Study in Tyranny*, New York, Konecky & Konecky, 1962.

Bullock, Alan, *Hitler and Stalin: Parallel Lives*, London, Fontana, 1998.

Cartier, Raymond. *La Seconde guerre mondiale*, Paris, Larousse, Paris-Match, 1965-1966.

Chaney, Otto Preston, *Zhukov*, Norman, University of Oklahoma Press, 1996.

Cowley, Robert (ed.) *No End Save Victory*, New York, G.P. Putnam's Sons, 2001.

*Descent into Nightmare*, Alexandria, Virginia, Time-Life Books, 1992.

Ellul, Jacques, *Autopsy of Revolution*, New York, Knopf, 1971.

Erickson, John, *The Road to Berlin*, New Haven, Connecticut, Yale University Press, 1999.

Fritzsche, Hans, and Hildegard Springer-Fritzsche, *Es sprach Hans Fritzsche: nach Gesprächen, Briefen und Dokumenten*, Stuttgart, Thiele, 1949.

Glantz, David M., *When Titans Clashed*, Lawrence, Kansas, Kansas University Press, 1995.

Gorodetsky, Gabriel, (Ed.), *Soviet Foreign Policy 1917-1991: a retrospective*, London, Frank Cass, 1994.

Hastings, Max, *Armageddon: the Battle for Germany, 1944-45*, New York, Knopf, 2004.

Irving, David, *Hitler's War*, London, Focal Point Publications, 2001.

Keegan, John, *The Second World War*, New York, Penguin, 1990.

Keitel, Wilhelm and Walter Görlitz, *The Memoirs of Field-Marshal Wilhelm Keitel*, New York, Cooper Square Press, 2000.

Kershaw, Ian, *Hitler 1936 – 1945 Nemesis*, New York, W. W. Norton & Company, 2000.

Konev, Ivan S., *Year of Victory*, Moscow, Progress Publishers, 1969.

Landemer, Henri, *La Division 'Charlemagne,' Les SS, L'Enfer Organisé (tome 2)*, Historia hors serie 21, 1971.

Lefevre, Eric, *Berlin, April 26, 1945: the 3rd company of the Sturmbatallion of the 'Charlemagne' division launch a counter-attack*, Militaria Magazine (July 1995), pp. 33-35.

Lewis, Jon E. (Ed.). *The Mammoth Book of How it Happened: World War II*, London, Robinson, 2002.

Mollo, Andrew, *The Berlin Führerbunker: The Thirteenth Hole*, After the Battle, No. 61, 1998.

Nolte, Ernst, *Der europäische Bürgerkrieg 1917-1945 Nationalsozialismus und Bolschewismus*, Berlin, Propyläen Verlag, 1987.

Nolte, Ernst, *Die faschistischen Bewegungen: die Krise des liberalen Systems und die Entwicklung der Faschismen*, Munich, Taschenbuch Verlag, 1966.

Overy, R. J, *Why the Allies Won*, London, Pimlico, 2002.

Payne, Stanley, *A History of Fascism, 1914-1945*, Madison, University of Wisconsin Press, 1995.

Pipes, Jason, *11.SS-Panzergrenadier-Freiwilligen-Division 'Nordland' and 33.Waffen-Grenadier-Division der SS 'Charlemagne'*, http://www.feldgrau.com/ accessed in 2005.

Reitsch, Hannah, *Flying is my Life*, London, Hutchinson & Co., 1954.

Ryan, Cornelius, *The Last Battle – Berlin 1945*, London, The New English Library Limited, 1967.

Salisbury, Harrison, *The Unknown War*, New York, Bantam Books, 1978.

Schmitt, Carl, *Der Begriff der Politische*, Munich, Duncker & Humblot, 1932.

Schmitt, Carl, *The Concept of the Political*, New Brunswick, New Jersey, Rutgers University Press, 1976.

Seaton, Albert, *The Russo-German War*, Novato, California, Presidio, 1993.

Seaton, Albert, *Stalin as Warlord*, London, Batsford, 1976.

Shtemenko, Sergei Matveevich, *The Soviet General Staff at War*, University Press of the Pacific, 2001.

Taylor, B., *She flew for Hitler!* Air Classics, February 1989.

Thorwald, Jürgen, *La grande fuga: incomincio alla Vistola, La fine all' Elba*, Firenze, Sansoni, 1964.

Thorwald, Jürgen, *Die grosse Flucht*, Stuttgart, Steingrüben Verlag, 1962.

Tieke, Wilhelm, *Tragödie um die Treue: Kampf und Untergang des III. (Germ.) SS-Panzer-Korps*, Osnabrück, Munin Verlag, 1968.

Trevor-Roper, Hugh R., *The Last Days of Hitler*, New York, Simon & Schuster, 1947.

*Victory in Europe*, Alexandria, Virginia, Time-Life Books, 1999.

Weber, Eugen, *Revolution? Counterrevolution? What revolution?*, Journal of Contemporary History, 9:2 1974 pp. 3-47.

Windrow, Martin, *The Waffen-SS*, London, Osprey, 2002.

Wulf, Josef, *Presse und Funk im Dritten Reich: Eine Dokumentation*, Frankfurt/Main u.a., Ullstein, 1983 (1966).

Zaloga, Steve, *Soviet Heavy Tanks*, London, Osprey-Vanguard, 1976.

Zaloga, Steve, *The Red Army of the Patriotic War (Men-at-Arms 216)*, London, Osprey, 1980.

Ziemke, Earl Frank, *Battle for Berlin: End of the Third Reich*, New York, Ballantine's, 1968.